**Collins**

# Collins School World Atlas

## Contents

COLLINS SCHOOL WORLD ATLAS
**Collins**
An imprint of HarperCollins Publishers
77-85 Fulham Palace Road
London W6 8JB

© HarperCollins Publishers 2010
Maps © Collins Bartholomew Ltd 2010

First published as Foundation World Atlas 2005, reprinted 2007
First published as Collins School Atlas 2008, reprinted 2008
New Edition 2010, reprinted 2010, 2011 (twice)

ISBN 978 0 00 732085 1

Imp 004

Collins ® is a registered trademark of HarperCollins Publishers Ltd

The contents of this edition of the Collins School World Atlas are believed correct at the time of printing. Nevertheless the publishers can accept no responsibility for errors or omissions, changes in the detail given, or for any expense or loss thereby caused.

British Library Cataloguing in Publication Data
A catalogue record for this book is available from the British Library.

Printed and bound in Hong Kong

All mapping in this atlas is generated from Collins Bartholomew digital databases. Collins Bartholomew, the UK's leading independent geographical information supplier, can provide a digital, custom, and premium mapping service to a variety of markets. For further information:
Tel: +44 (o) 141 306 3752
e-mail: collinsbartholomew@harpercollins.co.uk

Visit our websites at:
www.collinseducation.com
www.collinsbartholomew.com
www.collinsmaps.com

## A Political Map

Map A uses different colours to show clearly the shape of each country. A line is used to represent the international boundary around each country. It is possible to see the relative areas of the countries. Capital cities and other major cities are shown by symbols on a Political map.

## B Rainfall Map

The colours on Map B represent areas which have the same range of annual rainfall. From this type of map it is possible to find the wettest or driest region in a country. Rainfall maps are often accompanied by climate graphs such as the one shown at the bottom of the opposite page.

## Using Atlas Maps

An atlas includes different kinds of maps and diagrams. The different parts of an atlas page are shown on the map below which is a reduced version of page 28 in the atlas. In order to understand maps it is important to understand the labels and information which appear on each page. The example below is a reference map which

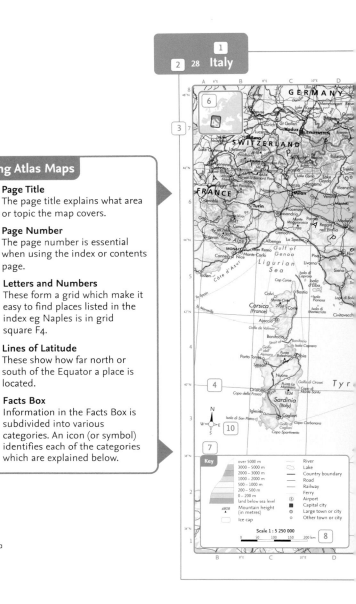

### Using Atlas Maps

1. **Page Title**
The page title explains what area or topic the map covers.

2. **Page Number**
The page number is essential when using the index or contents page.

3. **Letters and Numbers**
These form a grid which make it easy to find places listed in the index eg Naples is in grid square F4.

4. **Lines of Latitude**
These show how far north or south of the Equator a place is located.

5. **Facts Box**
Information in the Facts Box is subdivided into various categories. An icon (or symbol) identifies each of the categories which are explained below.

## Facts Box...

The information listed in the **Facts about**... box is explained below.

**Landscape:** Indicates the area and highest point.

**Population:** Lists the total population and the average number of people living in one square kilometre.

**Settlement:** Shows the percentage of the population living in cities and towns. The main towns and cities are also listed.

**Land Use:** Main crops grown and the main industries in the region are identified here.

**Development Indicators:** Four indicators are shown here.

**Life expectancy:** The number of years a newborn child can expect to survive.

**GNI per capita:** The annual value of production of goods and services of a country, per person.

**Primary school enrolment:** The total of all ages enrolled at primary level as a percentage of primary age children.

**Access to safe water:** Percentage of the population with reasonable access to sufficient safe water.

shows a variety of information such as settlement, communications, the physical landscape and political borders. In this atlas there are also many thematic maps which give information on one or two special topics. Maps A, B, C and D to the left and right of the reference map are typical examples of four different types of thematic map.

### C Relief Map

Map C shows the height of the land. Areas which are the same height above sea level are shown in the same colour. Lowland is shown in green and the highest mountain areas in brown or purple. The landscape features are named on a relief map and symbols are used to show the main mountain peaks. From this map we can see that Kilimanjaro is the highest peak in Africa.

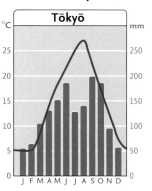

### Using Atlas Maps

**6   Locator Map**
The locator map shows the position of the map in a wider region.

**7   Key Box**
Every map has a key which explains the symbols used on the map. The use of symbols on the maps in this atlas are explained in more detail on page 6.

**8   Scale Bar and Ratio Scale**

**9   Lines of Longitude**
These show how far east or west of the Greenwich Meridian a place is located.

**10   Compass**
The compass shows the direction of north, south, east and west. Maps are usually drawn with north at the top of the page.

**11   Projection Note**

### D Population Map

The colours used on this map show the distribution of the population in the rural areas. Different sizes of dot show the distribution of cities and towns. Together the different colours and different size dots show where most of the people of Kenya live.

## Graphs

Information in this atlas is often presented as a graph or diagram. Three examples of graphs used are shown to the right.
**Pie graphs** are circles divided into segments to show percentage values.
**Bar graphs** can be used to compare production values of several topics.
**Climate graphs** are a combination of bars and lines.

### Pie Graph

- Forest
- Arable
- Pasture
- Other

15%
16%
14%
55%

### Bar Graph

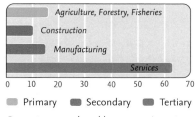

Percentage employed by economic sector

### Climate Graph

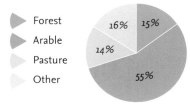

## Latitude and Longitude

**Lines of latitude** are imaginary lines which run in an east-west direction around the globe. They run parallel to each other and are measured in degrees, written as °. The most important line of latitude is the **Equator**, 0°. All other lines of latitude have a value between 0° and 90° North or South of the Equator. 90° north is the North Pole and, 90° south, the South Pole.

**Lines of longitude** are imaginary lines which run in a north-south direction between the **North Pole** and the **South Pole.** The most important line of longitude is 0°, the **Greenwich Meridian**, which runs through the Greenwich Observatory in London. Exactly opposite the Greenwich Meridian on the other side of the world, is the 180° line of longitude. All other lines of longitude are measured in degrees east or west of 0°.

When both lines of latitude and longitude are drawn on a map they form a grid. It is easy to find a place on the map if the latitude and longitude values are known. The point of intersection of the line of latitude and the line of longitude locates the place exactly.

The Equator can be used to divide the globe into two halves. Land north of the Equator is the **Northern Hemisphere.** Land south of the Equator is the **Southern Hemisphere.** The 0° and 180° lines of longitude can also be used to divide the globe into two halves, the **Western** and **Eastern Hemispheres.** Together, the Equator and 0° and 180°, divide the world into four areas, for example, North America is in the Northern Hemisphere and the Western Hemisphere.

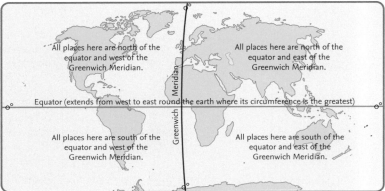

## Using Scale

The **scale** of each map in this atlas is shown in two ways:

1 The **Ratio scale** is written, for example, as 1 : 1 000 000.
  This means that one unit of measurement on the map represents 1 000 000 of the same unit on the ground.

eg **Scale 1 : 1 000 000**

2 The **line** or **bar scale** shows the scale as a line with the distance on the ground marked at intervals along the line.

## Different Scales

The three maps to the right cover the same area of the page but are at different scales. Map A is a large scale map which shows a small area in detail. Map C is a small scale map which means it shows a larger area in the same space as Map A, however in much less detail. The area of Map A is highlighted on maps B and C. As the scale ratio increases the map becomes smaller.

---

**1 The Globe**

**2 Lines of Latitude**

**3 Lines of Longitude**

**4 Lines of Latitude and Longitude**

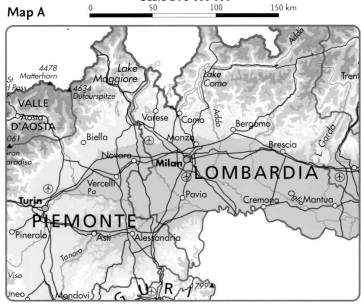

**Scale 1 : 3 000 000**

| 0 | 50 | 100 | 150 km |

**Map A**

## Mapping the world

To show the world on a flat map we need to peel the surface of the globe and flatten it out. There are many different methods of altering the shape of the earth so that it can be mapped on an atlas page. These methods are called **projections**.

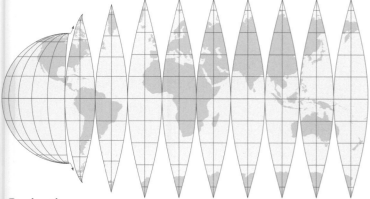

## Projections

Map projections change the shape and size of the continents and oceans. The projection used for world maps in this atlas is called Eckert IV. How the world map looks, depends on which continents are at the centre of the map.

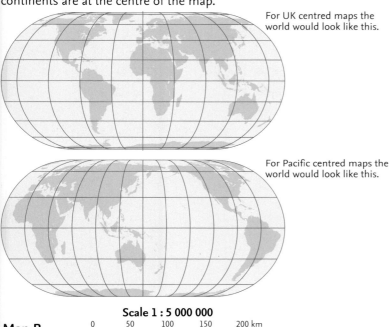

For UK centred maps the world would look like this.

For Pacific centred maps the world would look like this.

### Map B

**Scale 1 : 5 000 000**

0    50    100    150    200 km

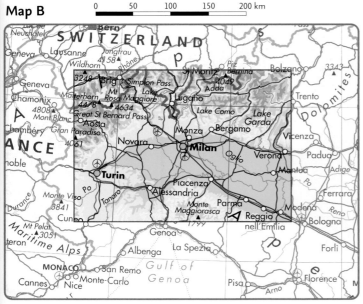

## Measuring Distance

The scale of a map can also be used to work out how far it is between two places. In the example below, the straight line distance between Brasília and Salvador on the map of Brazil is 7 cm. The scale of the map is 1 : 15 000 000. Therefore 7 cm on the map represents 7 X 15 000 000 cm or 105 000 000 cm on the ground. Converted to kilometres this is 1050 km. The real distance between Brasília and Salvador is therefore 1050 km on the ground.

**Scale 1 : 15 000 000**

0    150    300    450    600    750    900    1050    1200 km

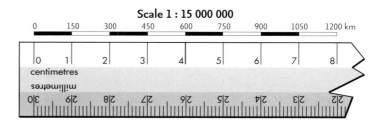

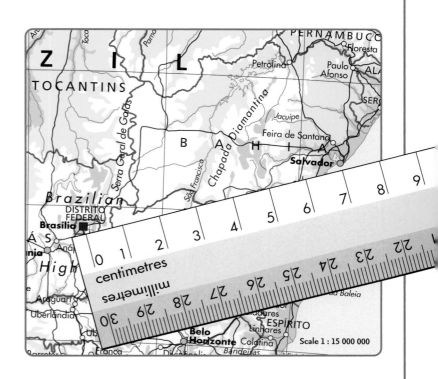

### Map C

**Scale 1 : 15 000 000**

0    200    400    600 km

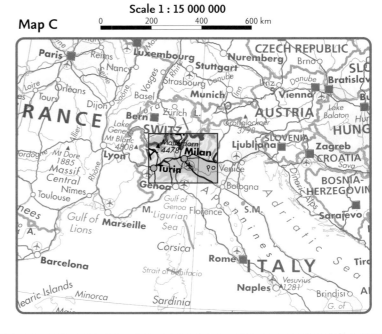

## Symbols

Maps use **symbols** to show the location of a feature and to give information about that feature. The symbols used on each map in this atlas are explained in the **key** to each map.

Symbols used on maps can be dots, diagrams, lines or area colours. They vary in colour, size and shape. The numbered captions to the map below help explain some of the symbols used on the maps in this atlas.

Different styles of type are also used to show differences between features, for example, country names are shown in large bold capitals, small water features, rivers and lakes in small italics.

## Using Grids

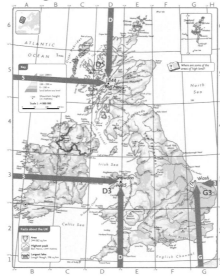

The map on the left shows the British Isles. Lines of latitude and longitude are numbered in 2° intervals in the map frame. These form a **grid** on the map. Large letters and numbers, together known as **alphanumerics,** are used to label the horizontal and vertical columns made by the grid.

The alphanumerics can be used to identify the **grid square** in which a feature is located, for example

> Ben Nevis is in D5,
> Snowdon in D3,
> The Wash in G3.

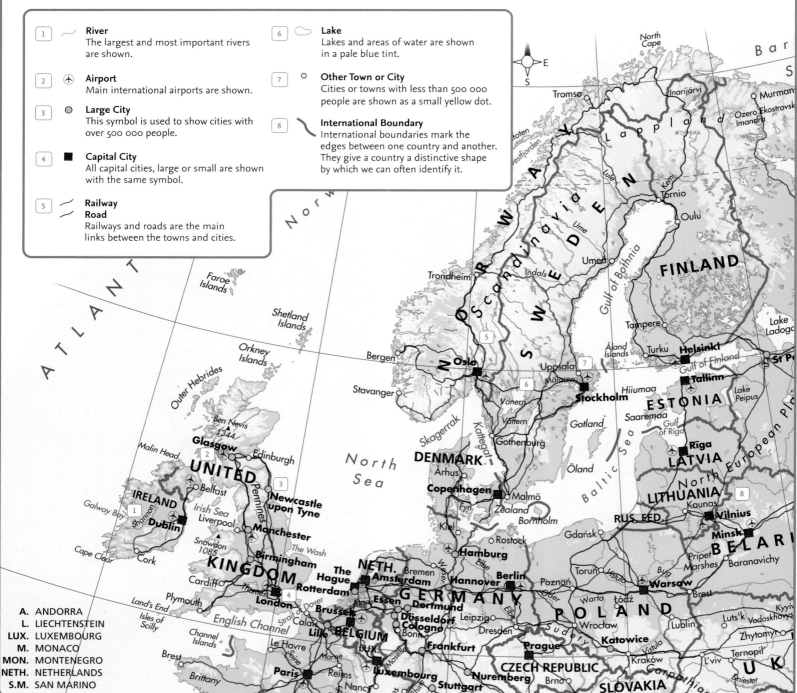

| | | | |
|---|---|---|---|
| 1 | River | The largest and most important rivers are shown. | |
| 2 | Airport | Main international airports are shown. | |
| 3 | Large City | This symbol is used to show cities with over 500 000 people. | |
| 4 | Capital City | All capital cities, large or small are shown with the same symbol. | |
| 5 | Railway / Road | Railways and roads are the main links between the towns and cities. | |
| 6 | Lake | Lakes and areas of water are shown in a pale blue tint. | |
| 7 | Other Town or City | Cities or towns with less than 500 000 people are shown as a small yellow dot. | |
| 8 | International Boundary | International boundaries mark the edges between one country and another. They give a country a distinctive shape by which we can often identify it. | |

A. ANDORRA
L. LIECHTENSTEIN
LUX. LUXEMBOURG
M. MONACO
MON. MONTENEGRO
NETH. NETHERLANDS
S.M. SAN MARINO

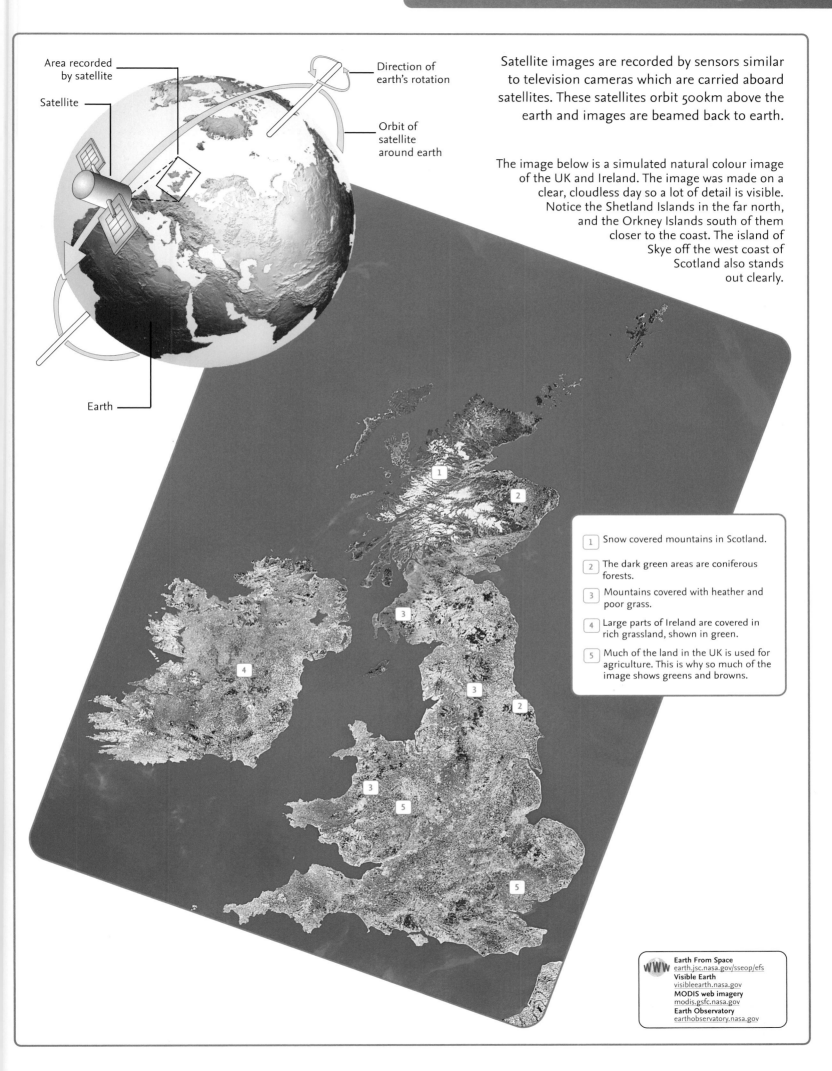

Area recorded by satellite

Satellite

Direction of earth's rotation

Orbit of satellite around earth

Earth

Satellite images are recorded by sensors similar to television cameras which are carried aboard satellites. These satellites orbit 500km above the earth and images are beamed back to earth.

The image below is a simulated natural colour image of the UK and Ireland. The image was made on a clear, cloudless day so a lot of detail is visible. Notice the Shetland Islands in the far north, and the Orkney Islands south of them closer to the coast. The island of Skye off the west coast of Scotland also stands out clearly.

1 Snow covered mountains in Scotland.

2 The dark green areas are coniferous forests.

3 Mountains covered with heather and poor grass.

4 Large parts of Ireland are covered in rich grassland, shown in green.

5 Much of the land in the UK is used for agriculture. This is why so much of the image shows greens and browns.

## What is GIS?

GIS stands for **Geographic Information System.** A GIS is a set of tools which can be used to collect, store, retrieve, modify and display spatial data. Spatial data can come from a variety of sources including existing maps, satellite imagery, aerial photographs or data collected from GPS (Global Positioning System) surveys.

GIS links this information to its real world location and can display this in a series of layers which you can then choose to turn off and on or to combine. GIS is often associated with maps, however there are 3 ways in which a GIS can be applied to work with spatial information, and together they form an intelligent GIS:

> **1. The Database View** – the geographic database (or Geodatabase is a structured database which stores and describes the geographic information.

> **2. The Map View** – a set of maps can be used to view data in different ways using a variety of symbols and layers as shown on the illustration on the right.

> **3. The Model View** – A GIS is a set of tools that create new geographic datasets from existing datasets. These tools take information from existing datasets, apply rules and write results into new datasets.

## Why use GIS?

A GIS can be used in many ways to help people and businesses solve problems, find patterns, make decisions or to plan for future developments. A map in a GIS can let you find places which contain some specific information and the results can then be displayed on a map to provide a clear simple view of the data.

For example you might want to find out the number of houses which are located on a flood plain in an area prone to flooding. This can be calculated and displayed using a GIS and the results can then be used for future planning or emergency provision in the case of a flood.

A company could use a GIS to view data such as population figures, income and transport in a city centre to plan where to locate a new business or where to target sales. Mapping change is also possible within a GIS. By mapping where and how things move over a period of time, you can gain insight into how they behave. For example, a meteorologist might study the paths of hurricanes to predict where and when they might occur in the future.

### GIS USERS

| | |
|---|---|
| The National Health Service | Environmental Agencies |
| The Police | Councils |
| Estate Agents | Supermarkets |
| Government Agencies | Insurance Companies |
| Schools | Banks |
| Emergency Services | Holiday Companies |
| The Military | Mapping Agencies |

## GIS Layers

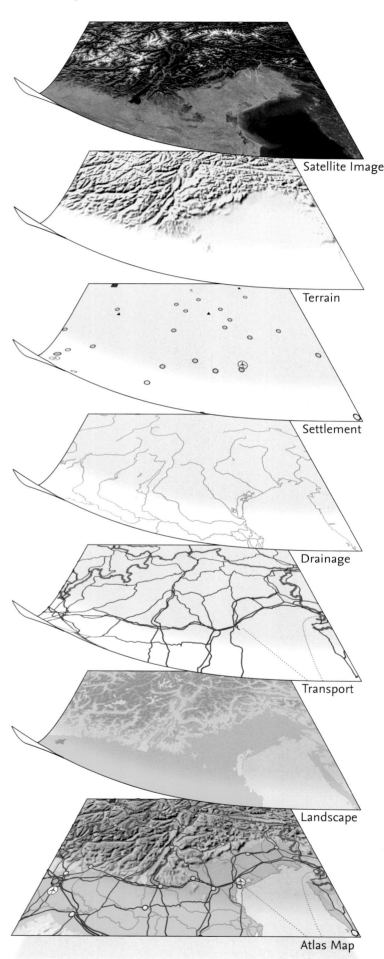

Satellite Image

Terrain

Settlement

Drainage

Transport

Landscape

Atlas Map

## Terrain

This map shows the relief of the country, and highlights the areas which are hilly in contrast to flatter areas. Relief can be represented in a variety of ways - contours and area colours can both show the topography. This terrain map uses shading which makes the hilly areas obvious.

## Energy Sources

This map illustrates the location of energy sources in the UK using point symbols. Each point symbol contains coordinate information and represents the different types of energy sources, for example the blue triangles show the location of wind farms. Points can be used to represent a variety of features such as banks, schools or shopping centres.

## Transportation

Roads shown here have been split into two categories, Motorways in green and Primary Roads in red, and these have been attributed with their road number. This is a road network using linear symbols. Rivers and railways could also be shown like this.

## Land Use

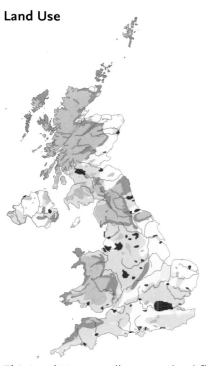

This Land Use map illustrates the different ways in which the land is used in areas across the UK. Each area is coloured differently depending on the type of land use. Areas in yellow are dominated by farms which grow crops, whereas urban areas are shown in red and forests in green. This map is used to show agricultural land use, but a similar map could be used to show different types of soils for example.

## Regional Migration

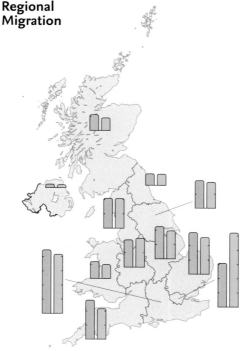

Graphs can be used on maps as a type of point symbol, and are an effective way of representing changes over time. This map has been divided into the regions of Britain and shows the number of people moving in and out of each region. The orange bar shows the number of people (in thousands) moving into an area, and the green bar shows the number of people moving out.

## Population Distribution

Population distribution can be shown on a map by using different colours for each category. This map uses 3 categories and each shows the number of people in a square kilometre. The yellow areas contain less than 10 people per square km; the light orange areas have 10 – 150, whilst the dark orange areas contain over 150 people per square km. The dark orange areas therefore have the highest population density.

## United Kingdom

SCOTLAND

Edinburgh

NORTHERN
IRELAND    Belfast

ENGLAND

London

WALES

Cardiff

IRELAND

## Facts about the United Kingdom

**Landscape**
Area: 244 082 sq km
Highest point: Ben Nevis 1344 m

**Population**
Total: 61 565 000
Density: 252 persons per sq km

**Settlement**
% Urban population: 90
Main towns: London, Birmingham, Manchester,
Leeds, Glasgow

**Land use**
Main crops: Wheat, barley
Main industries: Food products, machinery,
transport equipment, chemicals

**Development indicators**
Life expectancy: male 77, female 82
GNI per capita: US$ 33 630
Primary school enrolment ratio: 98
% Access to safe water: 100

### Key

| | International boundary |
| | National boundary |
| | Administrative boundary |
| ■ | Capital city |
| ○ | Administrative centre |

**Scale 1 : 3 000 000**

0  25  50  75  100 km

N
W   E
S

SHETLAND

Lerwick

ORKNEY

Kirkwall

WESTERN
ISLES

Stornoway

HIGHLAND

Inverness

SCOTLAND

ARGYLL
AND BUTE

Lochgilphead

MORAY

Elgin

ABERDEEN-
SHIRE

ABERDEEN
Aberdeen

ANGUS

Forfar

PERTH &
KINROSS

DUNDEE
Dundee

STIRLING

Stirling

Perth

FIFE

Glenrothes

EAST
LOTHIAN

Haddington

Dumbarton
RENFREWSHIRE
Paisley

Kilmarnock

Dunfermline
Alloa
Falkirk
7
6
Glasgow
4
Hamilton
Motherwell
SOUTH
LANARKSHIRE

8
9
Livingston
MIDLOTHIAN
10
Edinburgh Dalkeith

Newtown
St Boswells

SCOTTISH
BORDERS

NORTH
AYRSHIRE

Irvine

Ayr

EAST
AYRSHIRE

SOUTH
AYRSHIRE

DUMFRIES
AND GALLOWAY

Dumfries

NORTHUMBERLAND

Morpeth

Newcastle upon Tyne

Ballycastle

MOYLE

Ballymoney

BALLYMONEY

Coleraine
COLERAINE
Ballymena

Limavady
LIMAVADY
BALLYMONEY

Londonderry

### SCOTLAND
1. INVERCLYDE
2. WEST DUNBARTONSHIRE
3. EAST RENFREWSHIRE
4. GLASGOW CITY
5. EAST DUNBARTONSHIRE
6. NORTH LANARKSHIRE
7. FALKIRK
8. CLACKMANNANSHIRE
9. WEST LOTHIAN
10. EDINBURGH

### NORTHERN IRELAND
1. NEWTOWNABBEY
2. CARRICKFERGUS
3. BELFAST
4. CASTLEREAGH
5. NORTH DOWN

*What are the sub-regions of the UK?*

**ENGLAND**
1. MIDDLESBROUGH
2. READING
3. WOKINGHAM
4. BRACKNELL FOREST
5. WINDSOR & MAIDENHEAD
6. SLOUGH
7. THURROCK
8. MEDWAY

**WALES**
1. BLAENAU GWENT
2. MERTHYR TYDFIL
3. TORFAEN
4. CAERPHILLY

## Boroughs of Greater London

Barking and Dagenham
Barnet
Bexley
Brent
Bromley
Camden
City of London
Croydon
Ealing
Enfield
Greenwich
Hackney
Hammersmith and Fulham
Haringey
Harrow
Havering
Hillingdon
Hounslow
Islington
Kensington and Chelsea
Kingston upon Thames (admin. centre for Surrey)
Lambeth
Lewisham
Merton
Newham
Redbridge
Richmond upon Thames
Southwark
Sutton
Tower Hamlets
Waltham Forest
Wandsworth
Westminster

FRANCE
BELGIUM
IRELAND
ENGLAND
WALES

NORTHERN IRELAND

ISLE OF MAN

CHANNEL ISLANDS (UK)
ALDERNEY
GUERNSEY — St Peter Port
JERSEY — St Helier

Conic Equidistant projection

National Statistics Online
www.statistics.gov.uk
The Scottish Parliament
www.scottish.parliament.uk
Northern Ireland Office
www.nio.gov.uk
The National Assembly for Wales
www.wales.gov.uk

ATLANTIC OCEAN

North Sea

Where are some of the areas of high land?

Legend:
- over 1000m
- 500 – 1000 m
- 200 – 500 m
- 100 – 200 m
- 0 – 100 m
- land below sea level

▲ 1344 Mountain height (in metres)

Scale 1 : 4 000 000

**Facts about the UK**

Area
244 082 sq km

Highest peak
Ben Nevis, 1344 metres

Largest lake
Lough Neagh, 396 sq km

Fair Isle
Orkney Islands
Westray
Sanday
Stronsay
Mainland
Hoy
Pentland Firth
South Ronaldsay
Duncansby Head

Shetland Islands
Unst
Yell
Fetlar
Foula
Mainland
Bressay
Sumburgh Head
Fair Isle

Butt of Lewis
Cape Wrath
Thurso
Isle of Lewis
Clisham ▲ 799 Harris
St Kilda
Outer Hebrides
The Minch
Loch Shin
Dornoch Firth
North Uist
Skye
Moray Firth
Rattray Head
South Uist
Cuillin Hills 993
North West Highlands
Loch Ness
Spey
Deveron
Cairngorm Mts
Ben Macdui ▲ 1309
Dee
Don
Barra
Rum
Ben Nevis ▲ 1344
Grampian Mountains
Inner Hebrides
Coll
Ben More 966
Ben Lawers ▲ 1214 Loch Tay
Tay
Firth of Tay
Tiree
Mull
Loch Awe
Loch Lomond
Ochil Hills
Firth of Forth
Firth of Lorn
Loch Fyne
Forth
Jura
Firth of Forth
St Abb's Head
Islay
Clyde
Holy Island
Arran
Ayr
Southern Uplands
Tweed
Cheviot Hills
Malin Head
Mull of Kintyre
Firth of Clyde
Merrick ▲ 843
Nith
Tyne
Errigal ▲ 752
Foyle
Antrim Hills
Bann
North Channel
Mull of Galloway
Solway Firth
The Pennines
Tees
Erris Head
Donegal Bay
Lower Lough Erne
Lough Neagh
Lagan
St Bees Head
Scafell Pike ▲ 977
Eden
Lake District
North York Moors
Derwent
Achill Island
Lough Conn
Upper Lough Erne
Mourne Mts
Slieve Donard ▲ 852
Isle of Man
Flamborough Head
Lough Mask
Shannon
Dundalk Bay
Calf of Man
Morecambe Bay
Wharfe
Ouse
Spurn Head
Lough Corrib
Suck
Lough Ree
Boyne
Irish Sea
Ribble
Mersey
High Peak
Mouth of the Humber
Galway Bay
Liffey
Anglesey
Witham
Aran Islands
Lough Derg
Barrow
Nore
Wicklow Mts
Wicklow Head
Caernarfon Bay
Snowdon 1085
Dee
Trent
The Wash
Shannon
Suir
Cambrian Mountains
Wensum
Norfolk Broads
Little Ouse
Waveney
Dingle B.
Carrantuohill ▲ 1041
Blackwater
Lee
Cardigan Bay
Teifi
Severn
Avon
Great Ouse
Cam
Chelmer
St George's Channel
St David's Head
Wye
Severn
Cotswold Hills
Thames
Chiltern Hills
Cape Clear
Worms Head
886 Brecon Beacons
Avon
Thames
North Downs
Leith Hill ▲ 294
Celtic Sea
Carmarthen Bay
Bristol Channel
Mendip Hills
Salisbury Plain
Dungeness
Lundy
Exmoor
Avon
Test
South Downs
Hartland Point
Exe
Stour
New Forest
Beachy Head
Tamar
Yes Tor ▲ 619 Dartmoor
Lyme Bay
The Solent
Isle of Wight
Bodmin Moor
Bill of Portland
Land's End
English Channel
Isles of Scilly
Lizard Point

Lambert Azimuthal Equal Area projection

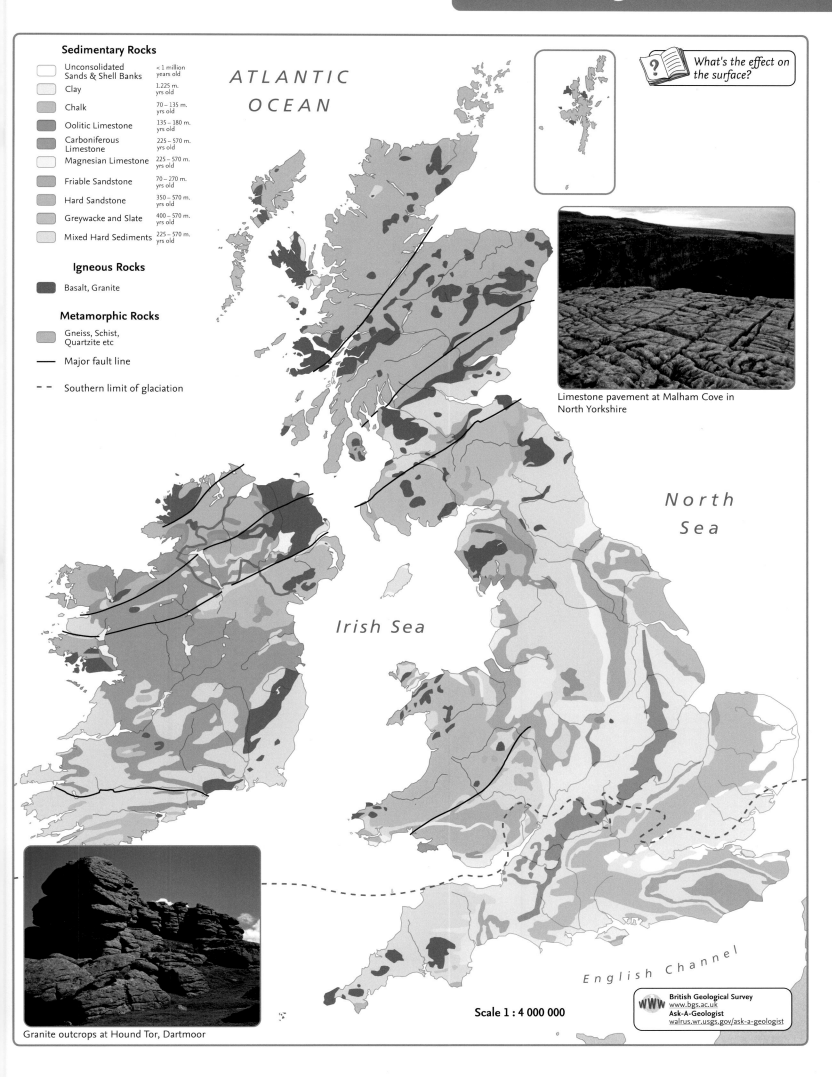

### Sedimentary Rocks

| | | |
|---|---|---|
| ☐ | Unconsolidated Sands & Shell Banks | < 1 million years old |
| ☐ | Clay | 1.225 m. yrs old |
| ☐ | Chalk | 70 – 135 m. yrs old |
| ☐ | Oolitic Limestone | 135 – 180 m. yrs old |
| ☐ | Carboniferous Limestone | 225 – 570 m. yrs old |
| ☐ | Magnesian Limestone | 225 – 570 m. yrs old |
| ☐ | Friable Sandstone | 70 – 270 m. yrs old |
| ☐ | Hard Sandstone | 350 – 570 m. yrs old |
| ☐ | Greywacke and Slate | 400 – 570 m. yrs old |
| ☐ | Mixed Hard Sediments | 225 – 570 m. yrs old |

### Igneous Rocks

☐ Basalt, Granite

### Metamorphic Rocks

☐ Gneiss, Schist, Quartzite etc

— Major fault line

-- Southern limit of glaciation

ATLANTIC OCEAN

North Sea

Irish Sea

English Channel

What's the effect on the surface?

Limestone pavement at Malham Cove in North Yorkshire

Granite outcrops at Hound Tor, Dartmoor

Scale 1 : 4 000 000

British Geological Survey
www.bgs.ac.uk
Ask-A-Geologist
walrus.wr.usgs.gov/ask-a-geologist

## Annual rainfall

There is little variation between winter and summer. The highest rainfall is in the west where winds from the sea blow against the mountains and hills. Central and eastern areas are more sheltered and have lower rainfall.

## Climate graphs and statistics

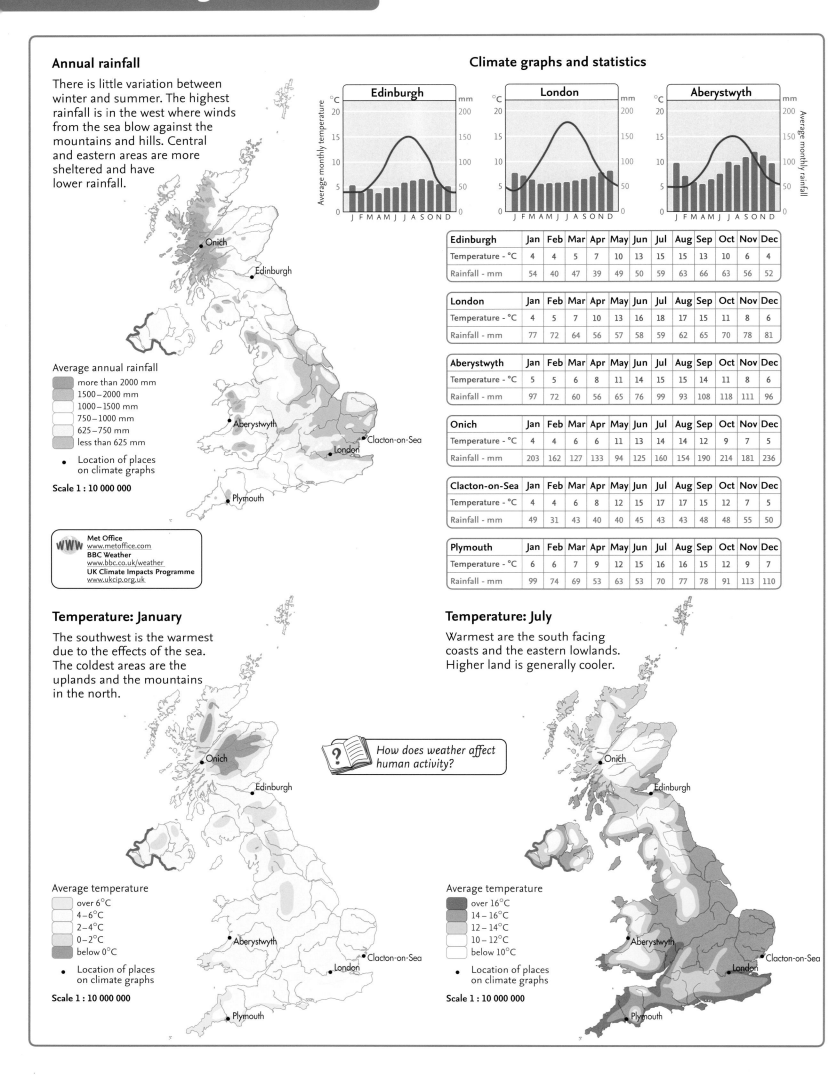

**Average annual rainfall**

- more than 2000 mm
- 1500–2000 mm
- 1000–1500 mm
- 750–1000 mm
- 625–750 mm
- less than 625 mm

• Location of places on climate graphs

Scale 1 : 10 000 000

**Met Office**
www.metoffice.com
**BBC Weather**
www.bbc.co.uk/weather
**UK Climate Impacts Programme**
www.ukcip.org.uk

| Edinburgh | Jan | Feb | Mar | Apr | May | Jun | Jul | Aug | Sep | Oct | Nov | Dec |
|---|---|---|---|---|---|---|---|---|---|---|---|---|
| Temperature - °C | 4 | 4 | 5 | 7 | 10 | 13 | 15 | 15 | 13 | 10 | 6 | 4 |
| Rainfall - mm | 54 | 40 | 47 | 39 | 49 | 50 | 59 | 63 | 66 | 63 | 56 | 52 |

| London | Jan | Feb | Mar | Apr | May | Jun | Jul | Aug | Sep | Oct | Nov | Dec |
|---|---|---|---|---|---|---|---|---|---|---|---|---|
| Temperature - °C | 4 | 5 | 7 | 10 | 13 | 16 | 18 | 17 | 15 | 11 | 8 | 6 |
| Rainfall - mm | 77 | 72 | 64 | 56 | 57 | 58 | 59 | 62 | 65 | 70 | 78 | 81 |

| Aberystwyth | Jan | Feb | Mar | Apr | May | Jun | Jul | Aug | Sep | Oct | Nov | Dec |
|---|---|---|---|---|---|---|---|---|---|---|---|---|
| Temperature - °C | 5 | 5 | 6 | 8 | 11 | 14 | 15 | 15 | 14 | 11 | 8 | 6 |
| Rainfall - mm | 97 | 72 | 60 | 56 | 65 | 76 | 99 | 93 | 108 | 118 | 111 | 96 |

| Onich | Jan | Feb | Mar | Apr | May | Jun | Jul | Aug | Sep | Oct | Nov | Dec |
|---|---|---|---|---|---|---|---|---|---|---|---|---|
| Temperature - °C | 4 | 4 | 6 | 6 | 11 | 13 | 14 | 14 | 12 | 9 | 7 | 5 |
| Rainfall - mm | 203 | 162 | 127 | 133 | 94 | 125 | 160 | 154 | 190 | 214 | 181 | 236 |

| Clacton-on-Sea | Jan | Feb | Mar | Apr | May | Jun | Jul | Aug | Sep | Oct | Nov | Dec |
|---|---|---|---|---|---|---|---|---|---|---|---|---|
| Temperature - °C | 4 | 4 | 6 | 8 | 12 | 15 | 17 | 17 | 15 | 12 | 7 | 5 |
| Rainfall - mm | 49 | 31 | 43 | 40 | 40 | 45 | 43 | 43 | 48 | 48 | 55 | 50 |

| Plymouth | Jan | Feb | Mar | Apr | May | Jun | Jul | Aug | Sep | Oct | Nov | Dec |
|---|---|---|---|---|---|---|---|---|---|---|---|---|
| Temperature - °C | 6 | 6 | 7 | 9 | 12 | 15 | 16 | 16 | 15 | 12 | 9 | 7 |
| Rainfall - mm | 99 | 74 | 69 | 53 | 63 | 53 | 70 | 77 | 78 | 91 | 113 | 110 |

## Temperature: January

The southwest is the warmest due to the effects of the sea. The coldest areas are the uplands and the mountains in the north.

**Average temperature**

- over 6°C
- 4–6°C
- 2–4°C
- 0–2°C
- below 0°C

• Location of places on climate graphs

Scale 1 : 10 000 000

*How does weather affect human activity?*

## Temperature: July

Warmest are the south facing coasts and the eastern lowlands. Higher land is generally cooler.

**Average temperature**

- over 16°C
- 14–16°C
- 12–14°C
- 10–12°C
- below 10°C

• Location of places on climate graphs

Scale 1 : 10 000 000

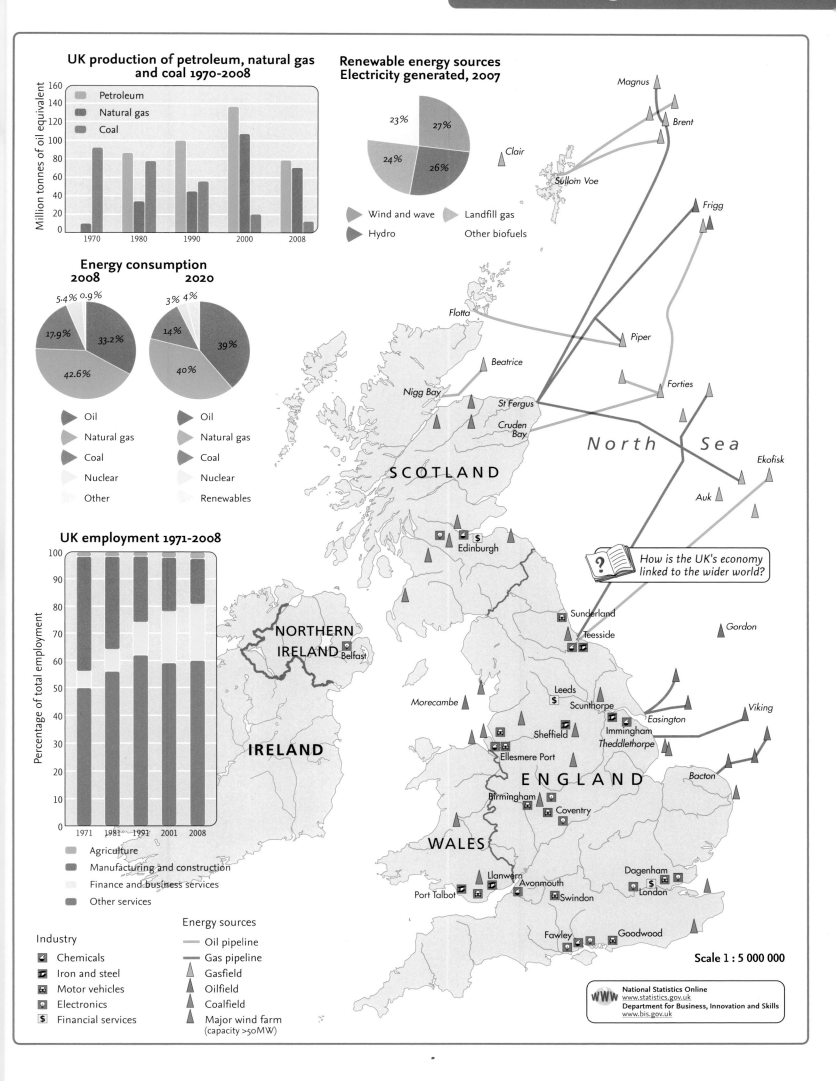

## UK production of petroleum, natural gas and coal 1970-2008

Million tonnes of oil equivalent

Petroleum
Natural gas
Coal

## Renewable energy sources
Electricity generated, 2007

27%
23%
26%
24%

Wind and wave    Landfill gas
Hydro    Other biofuels

## Energy consumption

**2008**

5.4%    0.9%
17.9%
33.2%
42.6%

Oil
Natural gas
Coal
Nuclear
Other

**2020**

3%    4%
14%
39%
40%

Oil
Natural gas
Coal
Nuclear
Renewables

## UK employment 1971-2008

Percentage of total employment

1971  1981  1991  2001  2008

Agriculture
Manufacturing and construction
Finance and business services
Other services

### Industry

- ☕ Chemicals
- ☕ Iron and steel
- ☕ Motor vehicles
- ☕ Electronics
- Ⓢ Financial services

### Energy sources

— Oil pipeline
— Gas pipeline
▲ Gasfield
▲ Oilfield
▲ Coalfield
▲ Major wind farm (capacity >50MW)

Magnus
Brent
Clair
Sullom Voe
Frigg
Flotta
Piper
Beatrice
Nigg Bay
St Fergus
Cruden Bay
Forties
*North    Sea*
Ekofisk
Auk
SCOTLAND
Edinburgh

*How is the UK's economy linked to the wider world?*

Gordon
Sunderland
Teesside
NORTHERN IRELAND
Belfast
Leeds
Morecambe
Scunthorpe
Easington
Viking
Sheffield
Immingham
Theddlethorpe
Ellesmere Port
IRELAND
ENGLAND
Bacton
Birmingham
Coventry
WALES
Llanwern
Dagenham
Avonmouth
London
Port Talbot
Swindon
Fawley
Goodwood

Scale 1 : 5 000 000

WWW  National Statistics Online
www.statistics.gov.uk
Department for Business, Innovation and Skills
www.bis.gov.uk

Congestion and pollution - what are the answers?

Country boundary
Internal boundary
Road
Railway
Ferry route
Airport
Capital city
Large town or city
Other town or city

Scale 1 : 4 000 000

ATLANTIC OCEAN

North Sea

Irish Sea

English Channel

SCOTLAND

NORTHERN IRELAND

IRELAND

ENGLAND

WALES

FRANCE

Shetland Islands

Lerwick
Scandinavia
Kirkwall
Aberdeen

Lerwick

Stromness  Kirkwall
Thurso
Wick
Stornoway
Tarbert
Ullapool
Lochmaddy
Uig
Inverness
Portree
Lochboisdale
Aberdeen
Fort William
Tobermory
Perth  Dundee
Oban
Stirling
Glasgow  Edinburgh  Berwick-upon-Tweed
Ardrossan
Brodick  Troon
Ayr
Morpeth
Dumfries
Cairnryan  Newcastle upon Tyne  Sunderland
Stranraer  Carlisle  Durham
Workington  Darlington  Middlesbrough
Coleraine
Londonderry  Scarborough
Larne
Donegal  Douglas  Harrogate
Ballina  Sligo  Enniskillen  Belfast  Heysham  Lancaster  York  Kingston upon Hull
Lisburn  Blackpool  Bradford  Leeds
Newry  Preston  Blackburn  Huddersfield
Westport  Dundalk  Bolton  Manchester  Doncaster  Grimsby
Drogheda  Liverpool  Stockport  Sheffield  Lincoln
Galway  Chester
Dublin  Stoke-on-Trent
Holyhead  Crewe  Derby  Nottingham
Wicklow  Caernarfon  King's Lynn  Norwich
Shrewsbury  Peterborough  Great Yarmouth
Limerick  Telford  Wolverhampton
Tralee  Birmingham  Coventry  Northampton  Cambridge
Waterford  Warwick  Ipswich
Wexford  Hereford  Luton  Harwich
Rosslare  Aberystwyth  Gloucester  Oxford  Watford  Felixstowe
Cork  Swindon  Slough  London
Fishguard  Newport  Reading  Southend-on-Sea
Pembroke  Cardiff  Bristol  Croydon  Ramsgate
Swansea  Bath  Ashford  Dover
Bridgend  Salisbury  Crawley  Folkestone
Taunton  Brighton  Hastings  Calais
Southampton  Newhaven  Eastbourne  Boulogne-sur-Mer
Exeter  Poole  Portsmouth
Weymouth  Bournemouth
Torquay  English Channel
Plymouth  Channel Islands
Penzance  Dieppe
Roscoff  Santander
Cherbourg  Le Havre  Rouen

Zeebrugge
Scandinavia  Amsterdam
Rotterdam  Zeebrugge
Scandinavia  Hamburg  Hoek van Holland

National Statistics Online
www.statistics.gov.uk
Department for Transport
www.dft.gov.uk
UK Snapshot
www.statistics.gov.uk/glance

## Population density

The greatest concentration of population in the United Kingdom is found in the areas immediately surrounding London where the number of persons per square kilometre is more than 500 times greater than in the Scottish Highlands. The total population of England is greater than the sum of the populations of Scotland, Wales and Northern Ireland.

**Persons per sq km**
- over 150
- 10 – 150
- 0 – 10

**Cities and towns**
- over 5 000 000
- 1 000 000 – 5 000 000
- 500 000 – 1 000 000
- 100 000 – 500 000
- 20 000 – 100 000

**Scale 1 : 5 000 000**

*Why do we live here?*
*Why do we not live there?*

### Population by country 2006

- England
- Scotland
- Wales
- Northern Ireland

4.9%  2.9%
8.4%
83.8%

2006 UK total 60 587 000
2011 Projected total 62 761 000

### Increase in population 1901-2031

*Dotted line indicates projected population*

Population in millions

80
70
60
50
40
30
20
10

1901 1911 1921 1931 1951 1961 1971 1981 2001 2011 2021 2031

- United Kingdom
- England
- Scotland
- Wales
- Northern Ireland

SCOTLAND

Glasgow

NORTHERN IRELAND

IRELAND

Dublin

Newcastle upon Tyne

Leeds

Liverpool
Manchester

WALES

Birmingham

E N G L A N D

London

### Population structure 2010

Percentage

100
90
80
70
60
50
40
30
20
10
0

**Age group**
- 65 and over
- 45 – 64
- 25 – 44
- 15 – 24
- 0 – 14

Males    Females

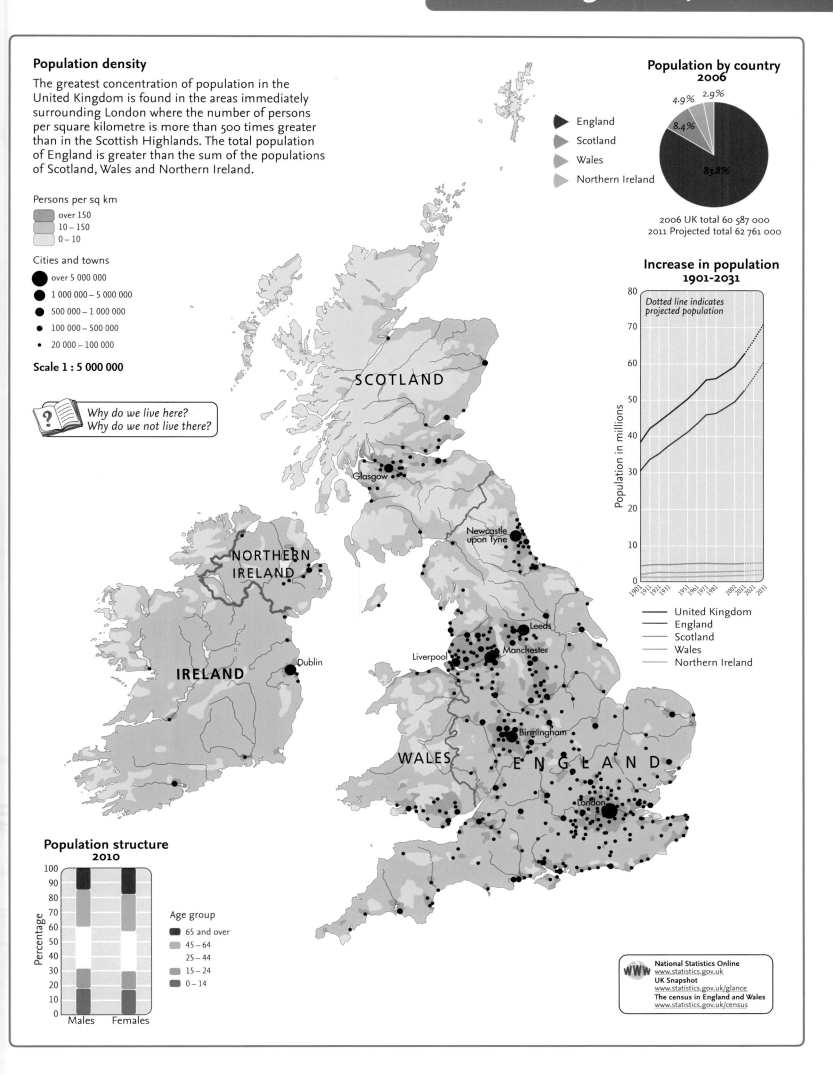

## Legend

- National Park
- Area of Outstanding Natural Beauty (England, Wales & N. Ireland)
  National Scenic Areas (Scotland)
- Heritage Coast (England and Wales)
  Preferred Conservation Zone (Scotland)
- ▲ World Heritage Site
- ● Major tourist attractions
  (over 1 million visitors)
- ○ Other tourist attractions

WWW **National Statistics Online**
www.statistics.gov.uk
**UK at a glance**
www.statistics.gov.uk/glance
**Visit Britain**
www.visitbritain.com

How important is tourism
as an economic activity?

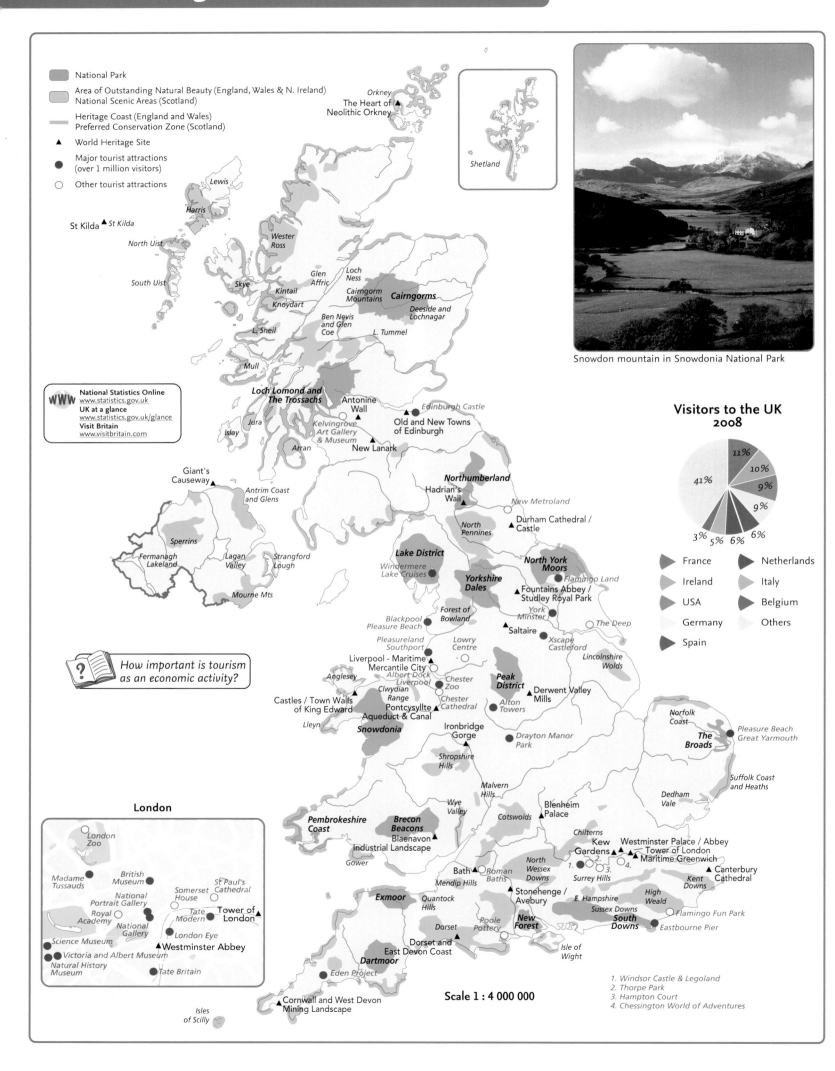

Snowdon mountain in Snowdonia National Park

### Visitors to the UK 2008

Pie chart percentages: 41%, 11%, 10%, 9%, 9%, 6%, 6%, 5%, 3%

- France
- Ireland
- USA
- Germany
- Spain
- Netherlands
- Italy
- Belgium
- Others

## Map labels

Orkney
The Heart of Neolithic Orkney ▲

Shetland

Lewis

Harris

St Kilda ▲ St Kilda

North Uist

South Uist

Wester Ross

Skye

Glen Affric
Loch Ness
Cairngorm Mountains
**Cairngorms**
Deeside and Lochnagar

Kintail
Knoydart
L. Sheil
Ben Nevis and Glen Coe
L. Tummel

Mull

Islay
Jura

Arran

**Loch Lomond and The Trossachs**

Antonine Wall
Edinburgh Castle ▲
Kelvingrove Art Gallery & Museum
**Old and New Towns of Edinburgh**
New Lanark ▲

Giant's Causeway ▲

Antrim Coast and Glens

Sperrins

Fermanagh Lakeland

Lagan Valley

Strangford Lough

Mourne Mts

**Northumberland**
Hadrian's Wall ▲

New Metroland ○
Durham Cathedral / Castle ▲

North Pennines

**Lake District**
Windermere Lake Cruises

**Yorkshire Dales**

**North York Moors**
Flamingo Land

Fountains Abbey / Studley Royal Park ▲
York Minster
Saltaire ▲

The Deep ○

Xscape Castleford

Lincolnshire Wolds

Blackpool Pleasure Beach
Forest of Bowland

Pleasureland Southport
Lowry Centre

Liverpool - Maritime Mercantile City
Albert Dock
Liverpool

Chester Zoo
Chester Cathedral

**Peak District**
Derwent Valley Mills
Alton Towers

Anglesey

Clwydian Range
Pontcysyllte Aqueduct & Canal
Castles / Town Walls of King Edward

**Snowdonia**

Lleyn

Ironbridge Gorge

Drayton Manor Park

Shropshire Hills

Norfolk Coast
**The Broads**
Pleasure Beach Great Yarmouth

Suffolk Coast and Heaths

Dedham Vale

Malvern Hills

Wye Valley

**Pembrokeshire Coast**

**Brecon Beacons**
Blaenavon Industrial Landscape

Gower

Bath
Mendip Hills
Roman Baths

Cotswolds

Blenheim Palace

Chilterns
Kew Gardens
1. 2. 3. 4.
North Wessex Downs
Surrey Hills

Westminster Palace / Abbey
Tower of London
Maritime Greenwich

Canterbury Cathedral
Kent Downs

**Exmoor**
Quantock Hills

Stonehenge / Avebury

E. Hampshire

High Weald

**South Downs**
Sussex Downs

Flamingo Fun Park
Eastbourne Pier

Dorset

Poole Pottery

**New Forest**

Isle of Wight

**Dartmoor**
Dorset and East Devon Coast

Eden Project

Cornwall and West Devon Mining Landscape

Isles of Scilly

**Scale 1 : 4 000 000**

1. Windsor Castle & Legoland
2. Thorpe Park
3. Hampton Court
4. Chessington World of Adventures

### London

London Zoo
Madame Tussauds
British Museum
National Portrait Gallery
Royal Academy
National Gallery
Science Museum
Victoria and Albert Museum
Natural History Museum
Somerset House
St Paul's Cathedral
Tate Modern
Tate Britain
Tower of London
London Eye
Westminster Abbey

## London 2012

In 2005 London won the bid to host the 2012 Olympic games. London previously hosted the Olympics in 1908 and in 1948, however, the size of the event in 2012 is enormous compared to the two previous games.

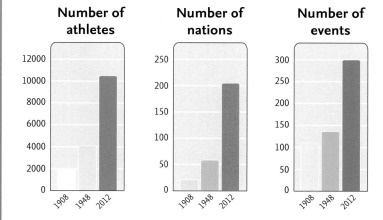

Number of athletes / Number of nations / Number of events

## How will London cope with such a huge event?

The Olympics is more than a sporting event. It is important that the planning of the games considers the effect on the environment and the benefits it will bring to the city not only in 2012 but for years after the games are over.

## The Olympic Park

The central location for the Olympics will be the Olympic Park, in the Lea Valley. By creating this park most of the venues and facilities can be centralised and within walking distance of each other.

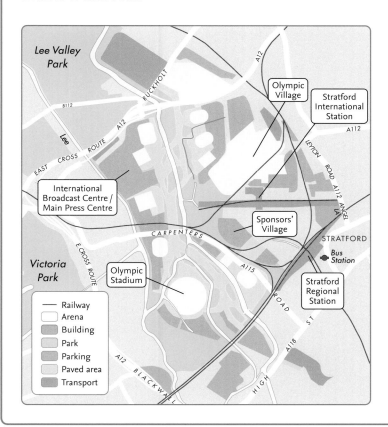

## Olympic venues around the UK

The Olympic Games
www.olympic.org
London 2012
www.london2012.com

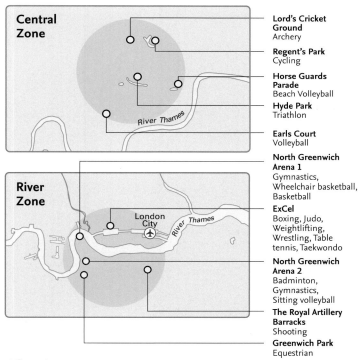

- Hampden Park football
- St James' Park football
- Old Trafford football
- Villa Park football
- Millennium Stadium football
- Weymouth sailing
- London Olympic Park athletics

*Will regeneration create sustainable communities?*

## Other London venues

**Central Zone**

- **Lord's Cricket Ground** Archery
- **Regent's Park** Cycling
- **Horse Guards Parade** Beach Volleyball
- **Hyde Park** Triathlon
- **Earls Court** Volleyball

**River Zone**

- **North Greenwich Arena 1** Gymnastics, Wheelchair basketball, Basketball
- **ExCel** Boxing, Judo, Weightlifting, Wrestling, Table tennis, Taekwondo
- **North Greenwich Arena 2** Badminton, Gymnastics, Sitting volleyball
- **The Royal Artillery Barracks** Shooting
- **Greenwich Park** Equestrian

## After the games

When the games are over the Olympic Park will be used as an urban park, the largest created in Europe for 150 years. Sports facilities and playing fields built for the games will be adapted for use by the local community. Some will be removed and relocated elsewhere in the UK.

## Map grid references (top and bottom): J I H G F E D C B A

## Longitude/Latitude labels
2°E · 1°E · 0° · 1°W · 2°W · 3°W · 4°W · 5°W · 6°W
56°N · 55°N · 54°N · 53°N

**North Sea**

N
W · E
S

**SCOTLAND**

Tobermory · Oban · Mull · Ben More 966 · Colonsay · Port Askaig · Islay · Port Ellen · Jura · Firth of Lorn · Loch Linnhe · Inveraray · Lochgilphead · Greenock · Rothesay · Bute · Arran · Brodick · Campbeltown · Mull of Kintyre

Pitlochry · Blairgowrie · Crianlarich · Ben Lomond 974 · Crieff · Perth · Dundee · Forfar · Arbroath · St Andrews · Firth of Tay · Tay · Loch Tay · Ben More 1174 · Callander · Ochil Hills · Kinross · Glenrothes · Kirkcaldy · Stirling · Dunfermline · Firth of Forth · Dumbarton · Clydebank · Glasgow · Paisley · East Kilbride · Hamilton · Motherwell · Livingston · Edinburgh · Dalkeith · Loch Lomond · Clyde · Forth · Kilmarnock · Irvine · Ayr · Prestwick · Biggar · Peebles · Galashiels · Dunbar · Coldstream · Jedburgh · Hawick · Ettrick Water · Teviot · Tweed · Southern Uplands · Sanquhar · Merrick 843 · Newton Stewart · Girvan · Stranraer · Whithorn · Nith · Moffat · Dumfries · Castle Douglas · Lockerbie · Solway Firth · Longtown · Carlisle

**North Channel** · Larne · Newtownabbey · Bangor · Belfast · Lisburn · Antrim · Lough Neagh · **NORTHERN IRELAND** · Newcastle · Downpatrick · Mourne Mts · Slieve Donard 852 · Antrim Hills

**IRELAND** · Skerries · Dún Laoghaire · Bray · Wicklow · Wicklow Head

**Irish Sea**

Isle of Man · Douglas

Berwick-upon-Tweed · Alnwick · Cheviot Hills · Morpeth · Newcastle upon Tyne · South Shields · Sunderland · Hartlepool · Tyne · Wear · Tees · Bishop Auckland · Durham · **Pennines** · Stockton-on-Tees · Middlesbrough · Darlington · Northallerton · Swale · Ure · Nidd · Whitby · North York Moors · Scarborough · Flamborough Head · Bridlington · North York · Ripon · Harrogate · Skipton · **Leeds** · Bradford · Halifax · Huddersfield · Barnsley · Beverley · Kingston upon Hull · Humber · Spurn Head · Cleethorpes · Grimsby · Goole · Scunthorpe · Doncaster · Rotherham · **Sheffield** · Chesterfield · Mansfield · Louth · Skegness · The Wash · Lincoln · Witham · Boston · Grantham · Nottingham · Derby · Trent · Derwent · York · Ouse · Selby

Penrith · Lake District · Scafell Pike 977 · Windermere 977 · Kendal · Keswick · Workington · Whitehaven · Barrow-in-Furness · Morecambe Bay · Morecambe · Lancaster · Ribble · Preston · Blackpool · Southport · Formby · Blackburn · Burnley · Rochdale · Oldham · Bolton · Wigan · St Helens · Warrington · Ellesmere Port · Mersey · Stockport · **Manchester** · **High Peak** · Macclesfield · Stoke-on-Trent · **ENGLAND** · Crewe · Chester · Mold · Clwyd · Dee · Wrexham · **Liverpool** · Birkenhead · Rhyl · Colwyn Bay · Bangor · Anglesey · Holyhead · Caernarfon · Caernarfon Bay · Snowdon 1085 · Llŷn Peninsula · Ffestiniog

Cromer · Norfolk

**Key**

| | |
|---|---|
| Country boundary | |
| Regional boundary | |
| Road | |
| Railway | |
| Airport | |
| Capital city | |
| Large town or city | |
| Other town or city | |

over 1000m
500 – 1000 m
200 – 500 m
100 – 200 m
0 – 100 m
land below sea level

▲ Mountain height (in metres)
1174
River
Lake

**Scale 1 : 2 000 000**

0 20 40 60 80 km

Conic Equidistant projection

FRANCE

WALES

Cambrian Mountains

English Channel

Bristol Channel

Cardigan Bay

St George's Channel

Channel Islands

Alderney
Guernsey
St Peter Port
Sark
Jersey
St Helier

Cherbourg
St-Lô
Coutances

Dieppe
Boulogne-sur-Mer

Strait of Dover

Lyme Bay

Isles of Scilly

Land's End

Lizard Point

Conic Equidistant projection

ATLANTIC OCEAN

SCOTLAND

Port Askaig · Jura
*Islay*
Port Ellen
Rothesay
*Bute*
Brodick
*Arran*
Irvine
Prestwick
Ayr
Girvan
Campbeltown
Mull of Kintyre
Stranraer
North Channel
*Firth of Clyde*

Malin Head

Bloody Foreland
Errigal ▲ 752
Letterkenny
Lough Foyle
Portrush
Coleraine
Londonderry
Strabane
Blue Stack ▲ 676
Donegal
Omagh
Bann
Ballymena
Antrim Hills
Larne

NORTHERN IRELAND
Antrim
Newtownabbey
Bangor
**Belfast**
Lagan
Lisburn

Donegal Bay

Lower Lough Erne
Enniskillen
Upper Lough Erne
Lough Neagh
Dungannon
Armagh
Monaghan
Newry
Downpatrick
Newcastle
Mourne Mts ▲ Slieve Donard 852

Erris Head
Belmullet
Sligo
Lough Allen
Cavan
Dundalk
Dundalk Bay

Irish Sea

Ballina
Lough Conn
Carrick-on-Shannon
Longford
Drogheda

Achill Island
Castlebar
Lough Mask
Roscommon
Lough Ree
Navan
Skerries

Westport
Claremorris
Boyne
Mullingar

Lough Corrib
Athlone
Suck
Lough

IRELAND

Galway
Galway Bay
Tullamore
**Dublin**
Dún Laoghaire
Bray

Connemara
Liffey
Naas
Wicklow Mts

Aran Islands
Lough Derg
Portlaoise
Wicklow
Wicklow Head

Ennis
Roscrea
Nenagh
Barrow

Kilkee
Kilrush
Limerick
Thurles
Nore
Kilkenny
Carlow
Arklow

Suir
Enniscorthy

Tralee
Tipperary
Clonmel
Carrick-on-Suir
New Ross
Wexford
Rosslare

Dingle
Cahir
Knockmealdown Mts
Waterford

Dingle Bay
Mallow
Blackwater
Fermoy
Dungarvan

Killarney
Carrantuohill ▲ 1041
Lee
Youghal

Boggeragh Mts
Sneem
Cork
Cobh

Bantry

Skibbereen
Old Head of Kinsale

WALES
Fishguard
St George's Channel

Mizen Head
Cape Clear

Celtic Sea

**Key**

| | |
|---|---|
| over 1000m | Country boundary |
| 500 – 1000 m | Regional boundary |
| 200 – 500 m | Road |
| 100 – 200 m | Railway |
| 0 – 100 m | ⊕ Airport |
| land below sea level | ■ Capital city |
| ▲ 1344 Mountain height (in metres) | ◉ Large town or city |
| ⌇ River | ○ Other town or city |
| Lake | |

Scale 1 : 2 000 000

0   20   40   60   80 km

Conic Equidistant projection

**Key**

- over 5000 m
- 3000 – 5000 m
- 2000 – 3000 m
- 1000 – 2000 m
- 500 – 1000 m
- 200 – 500 m
- 0 – 200 m
- land below sea level

Ice cap

▲ 5642  Mountain height (in metres)

**Scale 1 : 25 000 000**

0   250   500   750   1000 km

**Facts about Europe Relief**

**Area**
9 908 599 sq km

**Highest peak**
El'brus 5642 m

**Lowest point**
Caspian Sea -28 m

**Longest river**
Volga 3 688 km

**Largest lake**
Caspian Sea 371 000 sq km

Conic Equidistant projection

## European Union members

The European Union (EU) was created in 1957 by the Treaty of Rome. The original members of the then European Economic Community (EEC) were Belgium, France, West Germany, Italy, Luxembourg and the Netherlands. Since 1957 the EU has grown and now has 27 member states. The total population of the EU is now over 500 million.

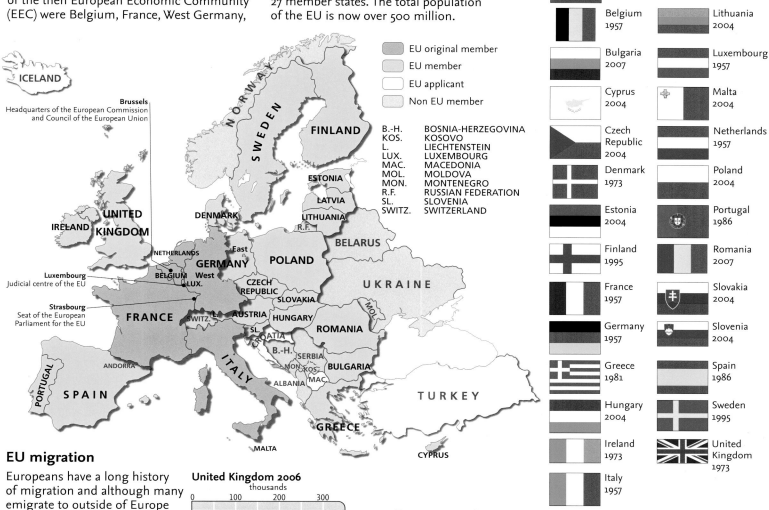

EU original member
EU member
EU applicant
Non EU member

| | |
|---|---|
| B.-H. | BOSNIA-HERZEGOVINA |
| KOS. | KOSOVO |
| L. | LIECHTENSTEIN |
| LUX. | LUXEMBOURG |
| MAC. | MACEDONIA |
| MOL. | MOLDOVA |
| MON. | MONTENEGRO |
| R.F. | RUSSIAN FEDERATION |
| SL. | SLOVENIA |
| SWITZ. | SWITZERLAND |

Brussels
Headquarters of the European Commission
and Council of the European Union

Luxembourg
Judicial centre of the EU

Strasbourg
Seat of the European
Parliament for the EU

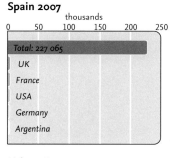

| | |
|---|---|
| Austria 1995 | Latvia 2004 |
| Belgium 1957 | Lithuania 2004 |
| Bulgaria 2007 | Luxembourg 1957 |
| Cyprus 2004 | Malta 2004 |
| Czech Republic 2004 | Netherlands 1957 |
| Denmark 1973 | Poland 2004 |
| Estonia 2004 | Portugal 1986 |
| Finland 1995 | Romania 2007 |
| France 1957 | Slovakia 2004 |
| Germany 1957 | Slovenia 2004 |
| Greece 1981 | Spain 1986 |
| Hungary 2004 | Sweden 1995 |
| Ireland 1973 | United Kingdom 1973 |
| Italy 1957 | |

## EU migration

Europeans have a long history of migration and although many emigrate to outside of Europe there is an increase in movement within the EU zone. EU citizens can travel, work and live in other member states with few restrictions. Most states have abolished passport and customs checks between members.

**United Kingdom 2006**
thousands
0   100   200   300

Total: 317 587
Australia
Spain
USA
France
New Zealand

**Netherlands 2006**
thousands
0  20  40  60  80  100  120  140

Total: 132 470
Belgium
Germany
UK
USA
Spain

**Spain 2007**
thousands
0   50   100   150   200   250

Total: 227 065
UK
France
USA
Germany
Argentina

**Poland 2007**
thousands
0  5  10  15  20  25  30  35  40

Total: 35 480
Germany
UK
USA
Ireland
Canada

**Lithuania 2007**
thousands
0        5        10        15

Total: 13 853
UK
Ireland
USA
Germany
Russian Federation

## Euro countries

In 2002 **euro (€)** bank notes and coins were introduced and 17 member states (the Eurozone) now use the **euro** as their official currency. There are 7 denominations of notes and 8 coins. It is likely that more members will adopt the **euro** in the future.

Eurozone
Non Eurozone
Non EU member

European Union
europa.eu
European Parliament
www.europarl.eu.int

A. ANDORRA
KOS. KOSOVO
L. LIECHTENSTEIN
LUX. LUXEMBOURG
M. MONACO
MON. MONTENEGRO
NETH. NETHERLANDS
S.M. SAN MARINO

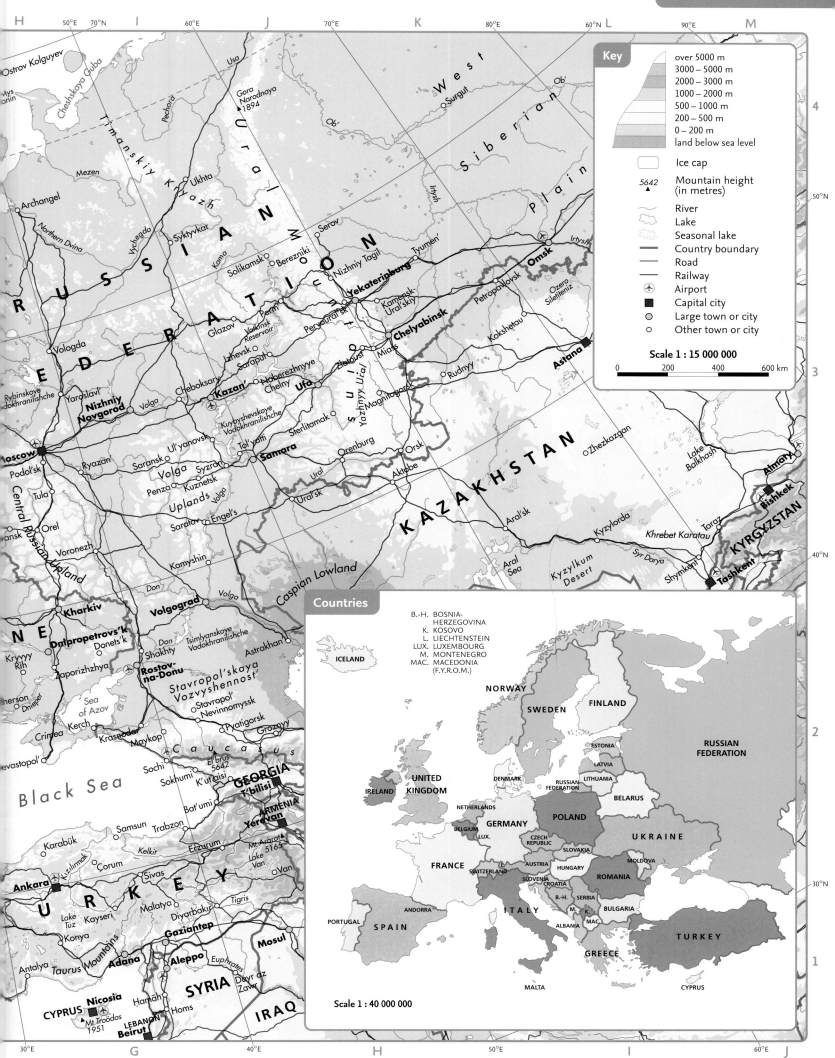

## Key

- over 5000 m
- 3000 – 5000 m
- 2000 – 3000 m
- 1000 – 2000 m
- 500 – 1000 m
- 200 – 500 m
- 0 – 200 m
- land below sea level

Ice cap

5642 ▲ Mountain height (in metres)

River
Lake
Seasonal lake
Country boundary
Road
Railway
✈ Airport
■ Capital city
⬤ Large town or city
○ Other town or city

Scale 1 : 15 000 000

0   200   400   600 km

## Countries

B.-H. BOSNIA-HERZEGOVINA
K. KOSOVO
L. LIECHTENSTEIN
LUX. LUXEMBOURG
M. MONTENEGRO
MAC. MACEDONIA (F.Y.R.O.M.)

ICELAND

NORWAY
SWEDEN
FINLAND
UNITED KINGDOM
IRELAND
DENMARK
ESTONIA
LATVIA
LITHUANIA
RUSSIAN FEDERATION
BELARUS
NETHERLANDS
GERMANY
POLAND
BELGIUM
LUX.
CZECH REPUBLIC
SLOVAKIA
UKRAINE
FRANCE
SWITZERLAND
AUSTRIA
HUNGARY
MOLDOVA
SLOVENIA
CROATIA
ROMANIA
ANDORRA
B.-H.
SERBIA
BULGARIA
PORTUGAL
SPAIN
ITALY
M.
K.
MAC.
ALBANIA
TURKEY
GREECE
MALTA
CYPRUS

Scale 1 : 40 000 000

### Map labels

West Siberian Plain

RUSSIAN FEDERATION

Ostrov Kolguyev
Mys ...anin
Cheshskaya Guba
Archangel
Northern Dvina
Mezen
Usa
Pechora
Gora Narodnaya ▲ 1894
Ob'
Surgut
Irtysh
Vychegda
Sykyvkar
Ukhta
Timanskiy Kryazh
Ural Mountains
Serov
Vologda
Kama
Solikamsk
Berezniki
Nizhniy Tagil
Tyumen'
Omsk
Irtysh
Yaroslavl'
Glazov
Perm
Yekaterinburg
Kamensk-Ural'skiy
Petropavlovsk
Astana
Rybinskoye Vodokhranilishche
Izhevsk
Votkinsk Reservoir
Pervoural'sk
Chelyabinsk
Kokshetau
Ozero Siletifeniz
Moscow
Podol'sk
Cheboksary
Kazan'
Naberezhnyye Chelny
Ufa
Miass
Zlatoust
Rudnyy
Nizhniy Novgorod
Volga
Kuybyshevskoye Vodokhranilishche
Magnitogorsk
South Ural
Kamensk-Ural'skiy
Tula
Ryazan'
Ul'yanovsk
Tol'yatti
Yuzhnyy Ural
Orenburg
Orsk
Zhezkazgan
Lake Balkhash
Almaty
Bishkek
Central Russian Upland
Orel
Saransk
Penza
Kuznetsk
Samara
Syzran
Volga
Ural
Aktobe
KAZAKHSTAN
Voronezh
Saratov
Engel's
Volga Uplands
Ural'sk
Aral'sk
Kyzylorda
Taraz
Khrebet Karatau
KYRGYZSTAN
Kamyshin
Caspian Lowland
Kyzylkum Desert
Shymkent
Tashkent
...nsk
Kharkiv
Don
Volga
Astrakhan
Aral Sea
Syr Darya
Volgograd
Tsimlyanskoye Vodokhranilishche
Krymskiy Rih
Dnipropetrovs'k
Donets'k
Don
Shakhty
Stavropol'skaya Vozvyshennost'
Zaporizhzhya
Rostov-na-Donu
Stavropol'
Nevinnomyssk
...herson
Dnieper
Sea of Azov
Kerch
Krasnodar
Maykop
Pyatigorsk
Grozny
Crimea
Caucasus
Sochi
El'brus 5642 ▲
...vastopol'
Sukhumi
K'ut'aisi
GEORGIA
T'bilisi
Black Sea
Bat'umi
ARMENIA
Yerevan
Samsun
Trabzon
Mt Ararat 5165 ▲
Karabük
Erzurum
Lake Van
Van
Kelkit
TURKEY
Kızılırmak
Corum
Sivas
Ankara
Kayseri
Diyarbakır
Tigris
Lake Tuz
Malatya
Konya
Euphrates
Gaziantep
Mosul
Taurus Mountains
Adana
Aleppo
Deyr az Zawr
Antalya
SYRIA
CYPRUS
Nicosia
Hamah
▲ Mt Troodos 1951
LEBANON
Beirut
Homs
IRAQ

Conic Equidistant projection

## Facts about Italy

### Landscape
**Area:** 301 245 sq km
**Highest point:** Mont Blanc 4808 m

### Population
**Total:** 59 870 000
**Density:** 199 persons per sq km

### Settlement
**% Urban population:** 68
**Main towns:** Rome, Milan, Naples, Turin

### Land use
**Main crops:** Sugar beets, corn, grapes
**Main industries:** Machinery, metal products, chemicals, food

### Development indicators
**Life expectancy:** male 78, female 84
**GNI per capita:** US$ 33 490
**Primary school enrolment ratio:** 99
**% Access to safe water:** 100

### Key
over 5000 m
3000 – 5000 m
2000 – 3000 m
1000 – 2000 m
500 – 1000 m
200 – 500 m
0 – 200 m
land below sea level

4808 ▲ Mountain height (in metres)

Ice cap

~ River
Lake
Country boundary
Road
Railway
Ferry
⊕ Airport
■ Capital city
● Large town or city
○ Other town or city

Scale 1 : 5 250 000

0    50   100   150   200 km

Lambert Conformal Conic projection

## Annual rainfall

Heaviest rainfall occurs during autumn and winter when westerly winds blow against the Alps and Apennines. Lowlands in the north and east have less rainfall because they are sheltered. The south has very little rainfall in summer.

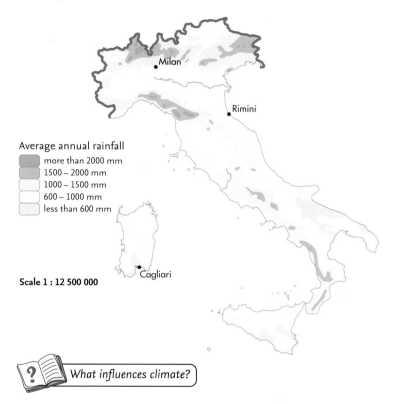

Average annual rainfall

- more than 2000 mm
- 1500 – 2000 mm
- 1000 – 1500 mm
- 600 – 1000 mm
- less than 600 mm

Scale 1 : 12 500 000

What influences climate?

## Climate statistics

The climate of Italy is greatly influenced by relief. The northern and central uplands have lower temperatures. Rainfall is higher to the west of the Apennines than to the east. Winters become milder and summers become hotter and drier as you move further south.

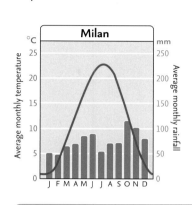

| Milan | Jan | Feb | Mar | Apr | May | Jun | Jul | Aug | Sep | Oct | Nov | Dec |
|---|---|---|---|---|---|---|---|---|---|---|---|---|
| Temperature - °C | 1 | 3 | 8 | 13 | 17 | 21 | 23 | 22 | 19 | 13 | 7 | 2 |
| Rainfall - mm | 52 | 49 | 65 | 70 | 85 | 89 | 55 | 71 | 72 | 114 | 101 | 80 |

| Rimini | Jan | Feb | Mar | Apr | May | Jun | Jul | Aug | Sep | Oct | Nov | Dec |
|---|---|---|---|---|---|---|---|---|---|---|---|---|
| Temperature - °C | 3 | 6 | 9 | 14 | 18 | 21 | 24 | 24 | 20 | 15 | 9 | 6 |
| Rainfall - mm | 64 | 36 | 68 | 71 | 57 | 57 | 71 | 61 | 61 | 93 | 114 | 79 |

| Cagliari | Jan | Feb | Mar | Apr | May | Jun | Jul | Aug | Sep | Oct | Nov | Dec |
|---|---|---|---|---|---|---|---|---|---|---|---|---|
| Temperature - °C | 10 | 10 | 12 | 15 | 19 | 23 | 25 | 25 | 23 | 18 | 14 | 12 |
| Rainfall - mm | 54 | 54 | 46 | 29 | 25 | 11 | 4 | 7 | 32 | 61 | 79 | 71 |

## Temperature: January

The mountains in the north and the central uplands can have very low temperatures. Northern lowlands are affected by cold winds from Europe. Coastal areas are the warmest.

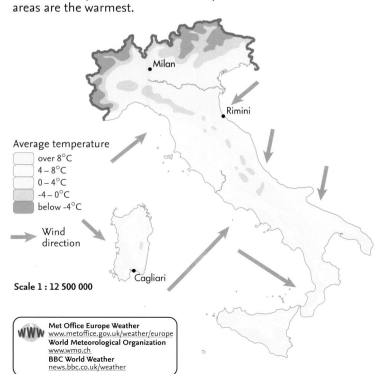

Average temperature

- over 8°C
- 4 – 8°C
- 0 – 4°C
- -4 – 0°C
- below -4°C

→ Wind direction

Scale 1 : 12 500 000

**Met Office Europe Weather**
www.metoffice.gov.uk/weather/europe
**World Meteorological Organization**
www.wmo.ch
**BBC World Weather**
news.bbc.co.uk/weather

## Temperature: July

Sheltered northern lowlands and coastal areas have hot summers. Other areas are cooler due to their altitude. In the south, hot, dry winds from Africa can lead to very high temperatures.

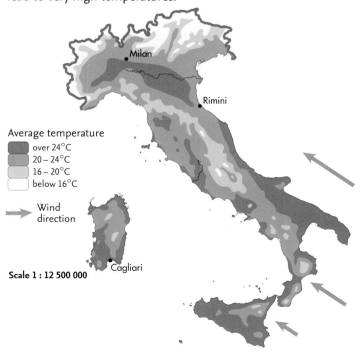

Average temperature

- over 24°C
- 20 – 24°C
- 16 – 20°C
- below 16°C

→ Wind direction

Scale 1 : 12 500 000

National Parks and Protected Areas have been created in Italy to preserve wildlife and natural vegetation. Most of these areas are inland. Despite its long coastline, Italy has very few protected coastal areas, with the exception of Cinque Terre Marine Protected Area which became a World Heritage Site in 1997. Pollution from oil spillage and industrial waste remains around the coast for long periods due to the low tidal movements of the Mediterranean Sea.

Alpine meadows in Gran Paradiso National Park

*Protected or polluted?*

Mont Blanc 4808
Val Grande National Park
Stelvio National Park
Lake Como
Dolomiti Bellunesi National Park
Lake Maggiore
Piave
Trieste
Gran Paradiso National Park
Milan
Lake Garda
Venice
Gulf of Venice
Adda
Oglio
Adige
Po
Turin
Parma
Ferrara
Reggio
Modena
Reno
Tanaro
Genoa
Bologna
Adriatic Sea
Cinque Terre Marine Protected Area
Cinque Terre National Park
Appennino Tosco-Emiliano National Park
Rimini
Gulf of Genoa
Florence
Arno
Monte Falterona National Park
Pisa
Ancona
Ligurian Sea
Arcipelago Toscano National Park
Ombrone
Tiber
Monti Sibillini National Park
Isola d'Elba
Grand Sasso and Monti d. Laga National Park
Pescara
Majella National Park
Rome
Abruzzo National Park
Gargano National Park
Asinara National Park
Arcipelago de la Maddalena National Park
Circeo National Park
Ofanto
Bari
Olbia
Alta Murgia NationalPark
Naples
Vesuvius 1281
Vesuvius National Park
Pontine Is
Bradano
Brindisi
Taranto
Tirso
Cilento and Diano National Park
Golfo di Orosei Gennargentu e Asinara National Park
Pollino National Park
Gulf of Taranto
Oristano
Sardinia
Tyrrhenian Sea
Cagliari
Sila National Park
Isole Lipari
Ionian Sea
Aspromonte National Park
Palermo
Reggio di Calabria
Mt Etna 3323
Sicily
Catania
Gela
Siracusa
Isola di Pantelleria
Areas at risk from industrial pollution
Coastal areas most at risk from oil pollution
Main tourist area
National Park
Protected Area
Scale 1 : 5 000 000

**World Heritage Site**

Cinque Terre Marine Protected Area was created to protect natural features. Unique rock formations and rare species of coral are found on the seabed. It is also a sanctuary for whales.

## Air pollutants

As in other developed countries it is in the main industrial areas of Italy that most harmful substances such as oxides of sulphur and nitrogen are released into the atmosphere. The main sources of these pollutants are power stations and car exhausts.

**Sources of pollutants**

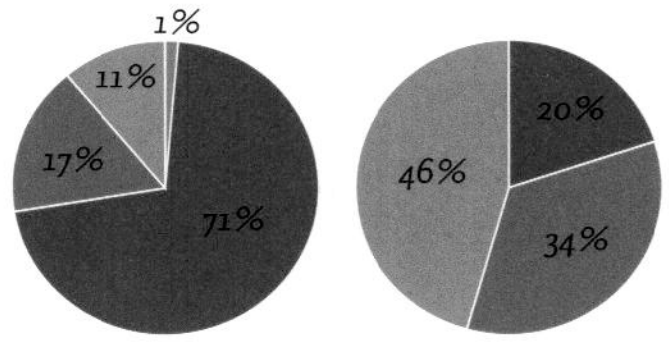
Transport
Manufacturing industries
Energy combustion
Other
Nitrogen oxides
1%
11%
17%
71%
Sulphur oxides
20%
46%
34%

WWW
**National Institute of Statistics** www.istat.it
**EUROSTAT** ec.europa.eu/eurostat
**The Italian Park Portal** www.parks.it

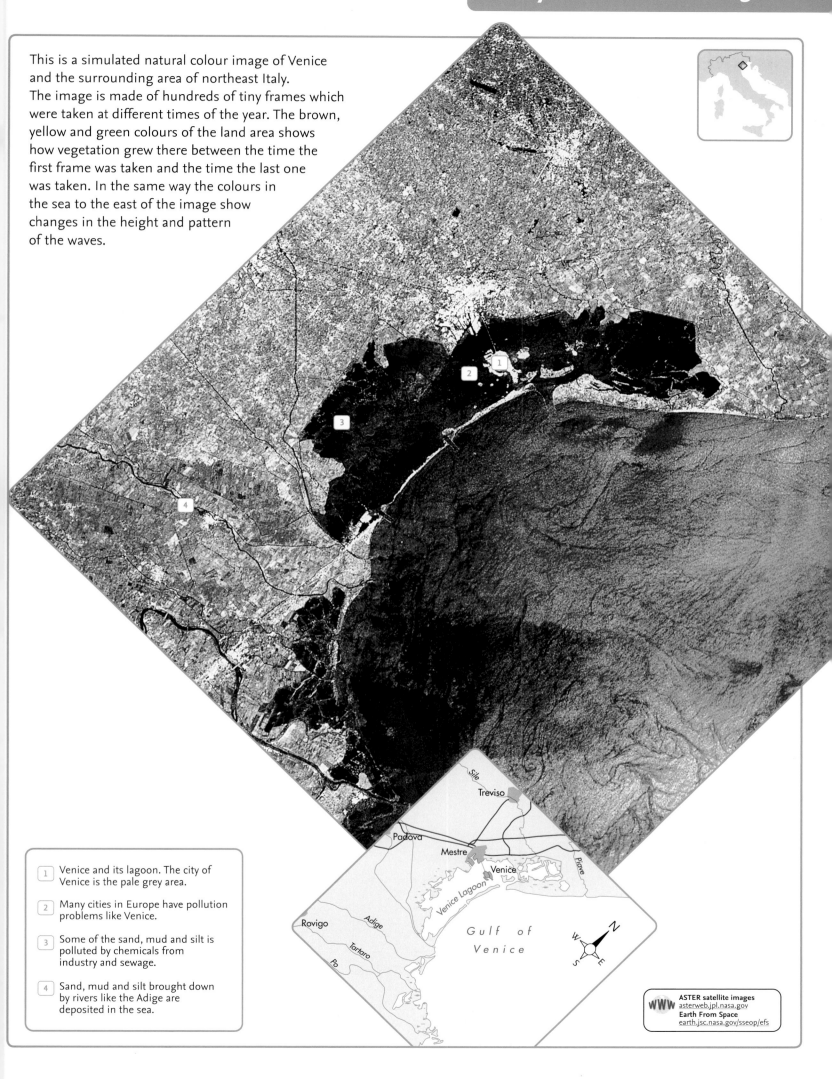

This is a simulated natural colour image of Venice and the surrounding area of northeast Italy. The image is made of hundreds of tiny frames which were taken at different times of the year. The brown, yellow and green colours of the land area shows how vegetation grew there between the time the first frame was taken and the time the last one was taken. In the same way the colours in the sea to the east of the image show changes in the height and pattern of the waves.

1. Venice and its lagoon. The city of Venice is the pale grey area.

2. Many cities in Europe have pollution problems like Venice.

3. Some of the sand, mud and silt is polluted by chemicals from industry and sewage.

4. Sand, mud and silt brought down by rivers like the Adige are deposited in the sea.

Treviso

Sile

Padova

Mestre

Venice

Piave

Venice Lagoon

Rovigo

Adige

Gulf of Venice

Tartaro

Po

N E S W

ASTER satellite images
asterweb.jpl.nasa.gov
**Earth From Space**
earth.jsc.nasa.gov/sseop/efs

Are there differences within the country?

N
W E
S

**Scale 1 : 3 000 000**
0   40   80   120 km

**Key**

3000 – 5000 m
2000 – 3000 m
1000 – 2000 m
500 – 1000 m
200 – 500 m
0 – 200 m

4808 ▲  Mountain height (in metres)
River
Lake
International boundary
Internal boundary
Road
Railway
✈  Airport
●  Large town or city
○  Other town or city

### Facts about Northern Italy

**Landscape**
Area: 97 756 sq km
Highest point: Mont Blanc 4808 m

**Population**
Total: 22 841 141
Density: 234 persons per sq km

**Settlement**
Main towns: Milan, Turin, Genoa

**Land use**
Main crops: Cereals, rice
Main industries: Electrical goods, cars

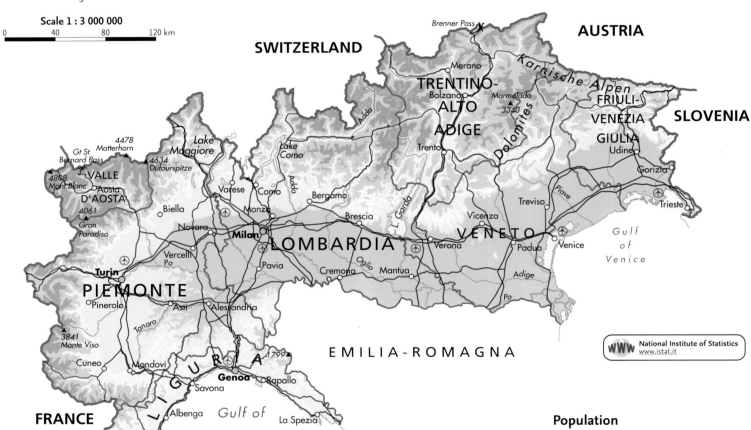

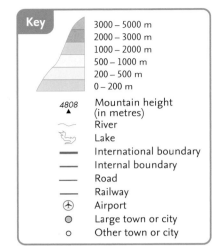

National Institute of Statistics
www.istat.it

Lambert Conformal Conic projection

### Population

Population distribution is uneven, high around the cities such as Milan and Turin, low in the mountains.

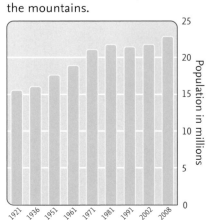

### Land use

The main industrial cities are in the west of the region. The fertile lowlands in the Po Valley produce wheat, maize and rice.

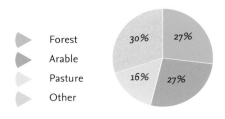

Forest
Arable
Pasture
Other

30%   27%
16%   27%

### Employment

The manufacture of consumer goods, especially cars and car components, dominates the region's economy.

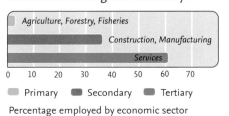

Agriculture, Forestry, Fisheries
Construction, Manufacturing
Services

0  10  20  30  40  50  60  70

Primary   Secondary   Tertiary

Percentage employed by economic sector

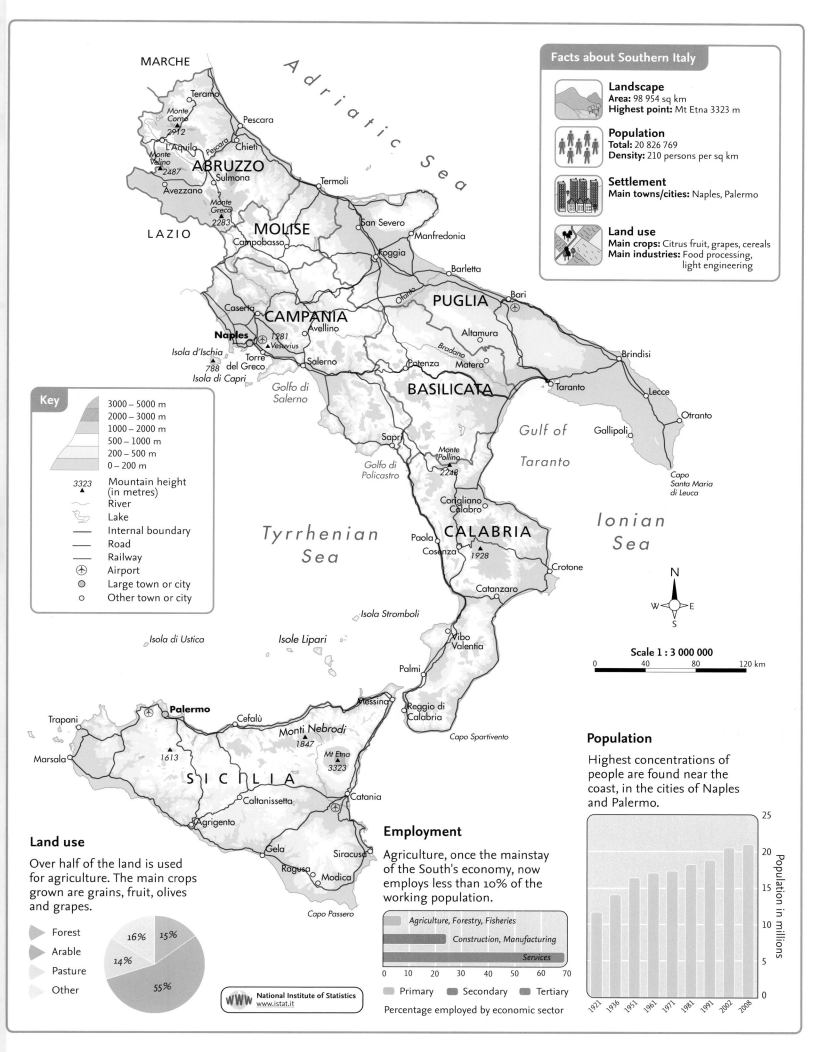

MARCHE

*Adriatic Sea*

Teramo
Monte Corno 2912
Pescara
L'Aquila
Monte Velino 2487
ABRUZZO
Chieti
Sulmona
Avezzano
Monte Greco 2283
Termoli
LAZIO
MOLISE
Campobasso
San Severo
Manfredonia
Foggia
Barletta
Bari
Caserta
CAMPANIA
Avellino
Altamura
Brindisi
Naples
1281 Vesuvius
Isola d'Ischia
Torre del Greco
788
Salerno
*Bradano*
*Ofanto*
PUGLIA
Potenza
Matera
Lecce
Isola di Capri
Golfo di Salerno
BASILICATA
Taranto
Otranto
Sapri
Golfo di Policastro
Monte Pollino 2248
Gulf of Taranto
Gallipoli
Capo Santa Maria di Leuca
Corigliano Calabro
*Tyrrhenian Sea*
Paola
Cosenza 1928
CALABRIA
*Ionian Sea*
Crotone
Catanzaro
Isola Stromboli
Isola di Ustica
Isole Lipari
Vibo Valentia
Palmi
Messina
Reggio di Calabria
Capo Spartivento
Trapani
Palermo
Cefalù
Monti Nebrodi 1847
Marsala
1613
Mt Etna 3323
Caltanissetta
Catania
S I C I L I A
Agrigento
Gela
Siracusa
Ragusa
Modica
Capo Passero

## Facts about Southern Italy

**Landscape**
Area: 98 954 sq km
Highest point: Mt Etna 3323 m

**Population**
Total: 20 826 769
Density: 210 persons per sq km

**Settlement**
Main towns/cities: Naples, Palermo

**Land use**
Main crops: Citrus fruit, grapes, cereals
Main industries: Food processing, light engineering

## Key

3000 – 5000 m
2000 – 3000 m
1000 – 2000 m
500 – 1000 m
200 – 500 m
0 – 200 m

3323 ▲ Mountain height (in metres)
River
Lake
Internal boundary
Road
Railway
✈ Airport
⬤ Large town or city
○ Other town or city

Scale 1 : 3 000 000
0    40    80    120 km

N
W    E
S

## Land use

Over half of the land is used for agriculture. The main crops grown are grains, fruit, olives and grapes.

▶ Forest
▶ Arable
▶ Pasture
▶ Other

15%
16%
14%
55%

**www** National Institute of Statistics
www.istat.it

## Employment

Agriculture, once the mainstay of the South's economy, now employs less than 10% of the working population.

Agriculture, Forestry, Fisheries
Construction, Manufacturing
Services

0   10   20   30   40   50   60   70

■ Primary   ■ Secondary   ■ Tertiary
Percentage employed by economic sector

## Population

Highest concentrations of people are found near the coast, in the cities of Naples and Palermo.

25
20
15
10
5
0
Population in millions

1921  1936  1951  1961  1971  1981  1991  2002  2008

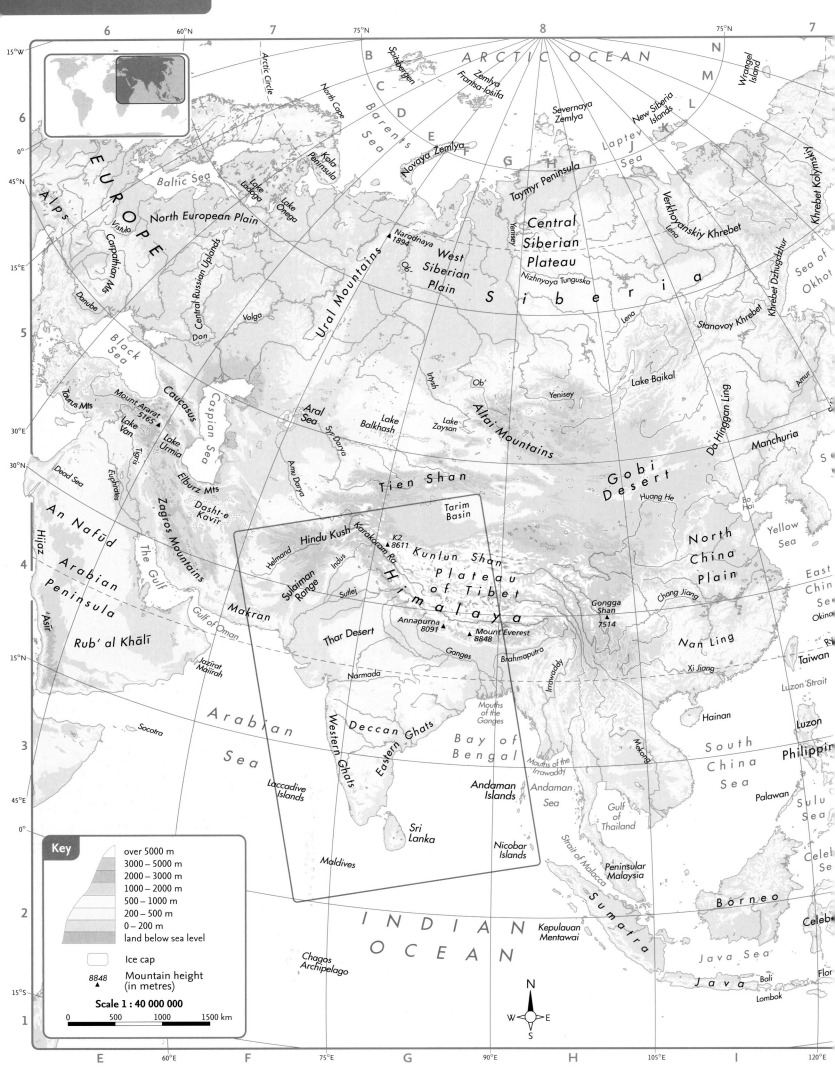

EUROPE

Alps

Carpathian Mts

Danube

Vistula

Baltic Sea

North European Plain

Central Russian Uplands

Volga

Don

Black Sea

Taurus Mts

Mount Ararat 5165 ▲

Lake Van

Caucasus

Lake Urmia

Tigris

Euphrates

Dead Sea

Hijaz

'Asīr

An Nafūd

Arabian Peninsula

Rub' al Khālī

Elburz Mts

Caspian Sea

Dasht-e Kavir

Zagros Mountains

The Gulf

Makran

Gulf of Oman

Jazīrat Maṣīrah

Socotra

Arabian Sea

Laccadive Islands

Maldives

Chagos Archipelago

Kola Peninsula

Lake Ladoga

Lake Onega

North Cape

Arctic Circle

Ural Mountains

Spitsbergen

Barents Sea

Novaya Zemlya

Zemlya Frantsa-Iosifa

Narodnaya 1894 ▲

Ob'

West Siberian Plain

Irtysh

Aral Sea

Syr Darya

Amu Darya

Lake Balkhash

Lake Zaysan

Tien Shan

Hindu Kush

Karakoram Ra.

K2 8611 ▲

Sulaiman Range

Helmand

Indus

Sutlej

Thar Desert

Narmada

Western Ghats

Deccan

Eastern Ghats

Sri Lanka

Severnaya Zemlya

Nizhnyaya Tunguska

Yenisey

Central Siberian Plateau

Taymyr Peninsula

Lena

New Siberia Islands

Wrangel Island

Laptev Sea

Verkhoyanskiy Khrebet

Khrebet Kolymsk...

Siberia

Lena

Stanovoy Khrebet

Khrebet Dzhugdzhur

Sea of Okhot...

Lake Baikal

Altai Mountains

Yenisey

Gobi Desert

Da Hinggan Ling

Manchuria

Tarim Basin

Kunlun Shan

Plateau of Tibet

Himalaya

Annapurna 8091 ▲

Mount Everest 8848 ▲

Ganges

Brahmaputra

Mouths of the Ganges

Bay of Bengal

Andaman Islands

Andaman Sea

Nicobar Islands

Mouths of the Irrawaddy

Irrawaddy

Huang He

Bo Hai

Yellow Sea

North China Plain

Chang Jiang

Gongga Shan 7514

Nan Ling

Xi Jiang

Taiwan

East China Sea

Okina...

Luzon Strait

Hainan

South China Sea

Mekong

Gulf of Thailand

Luzon

Philippi...

Palawan

Sulu Sea

Strait of Malacca

Peninsular Malaysia

Sumatra

Kepulauan Mentawai

Borneo

Celeb... Se...

Java Sea

Java

Bali

Lombok

Flor...

Celeb...

INDIAN OCEAN

### Key

- over 5000 m
- 3000 – 5000 m
- 2000 – 3000 m
- 1000 – 2000 m
- 500 – 1000 m
- 200 – 500 m
- 0 – 200 m
- land below sea level

☐ Ice cap

8848 ▲ Mountain height (in metres)

**Scale 1 : 40 000 000**

0    500    1000    1500 km

N
W   E
S

**Facts about Asia**

**Area**
45 036 492 sq km

**Highest peak**
Mt Everest 8848 m

**Lowest point**
Dead Sea -421 m

**Longest river**
Chang Jiang 6380 km

**Largest lake**
Caspian Sea 371 000 sq km

1. Sri Lanka is the large island off the southeastern coast of India. The bright colours show that it is mountainous especially in the southwestern part of the island.

2. The river Ganges enters the sea in the Bay of Bengal. The river can be seen as a thin blue line. Where the river enters the sea a large delta has formed.

3. The snow covered Himalayan Mountains stand out clearly in northern India.

4. The valley of the river Indus in Pakistan stands out on this image as a dark brown area.

**WWW** MODIS web imagery
modis.gsfc.nasa.gov
**Visible Earth**
visibleearth.nasa.gov

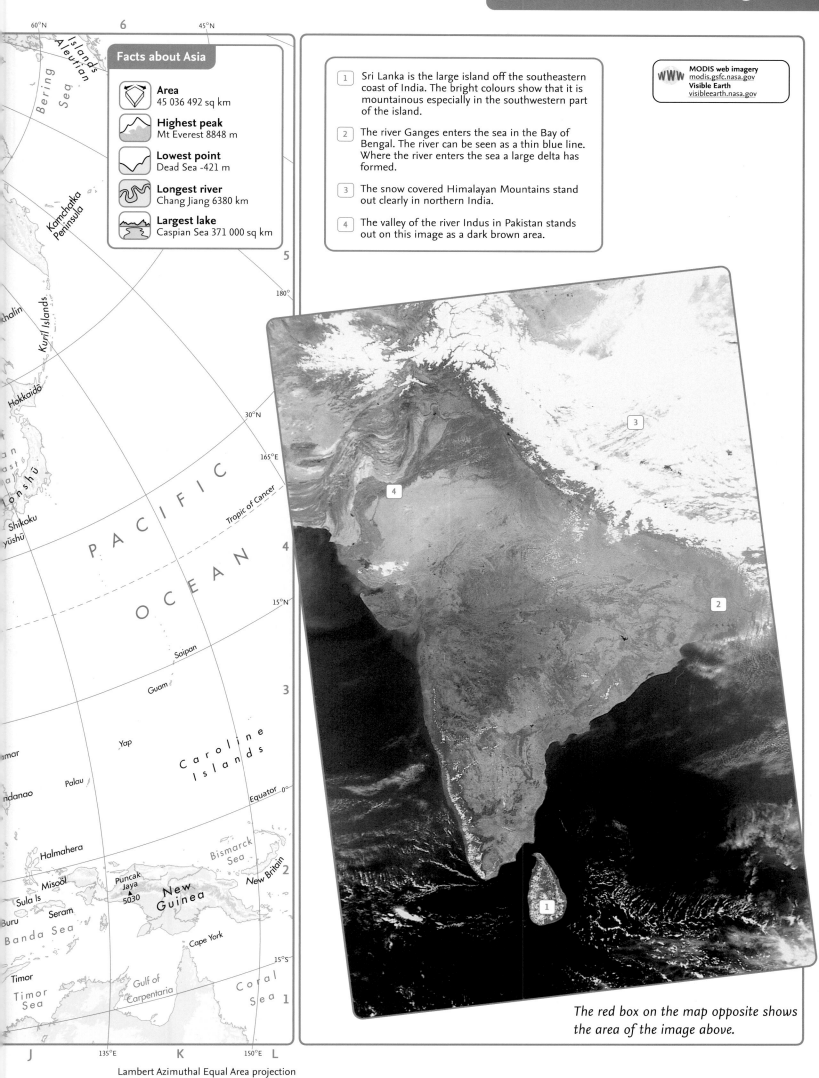

*The red box on the map opposite shows the area of the image above.*

Lambert Azimuthal Equal Area projection

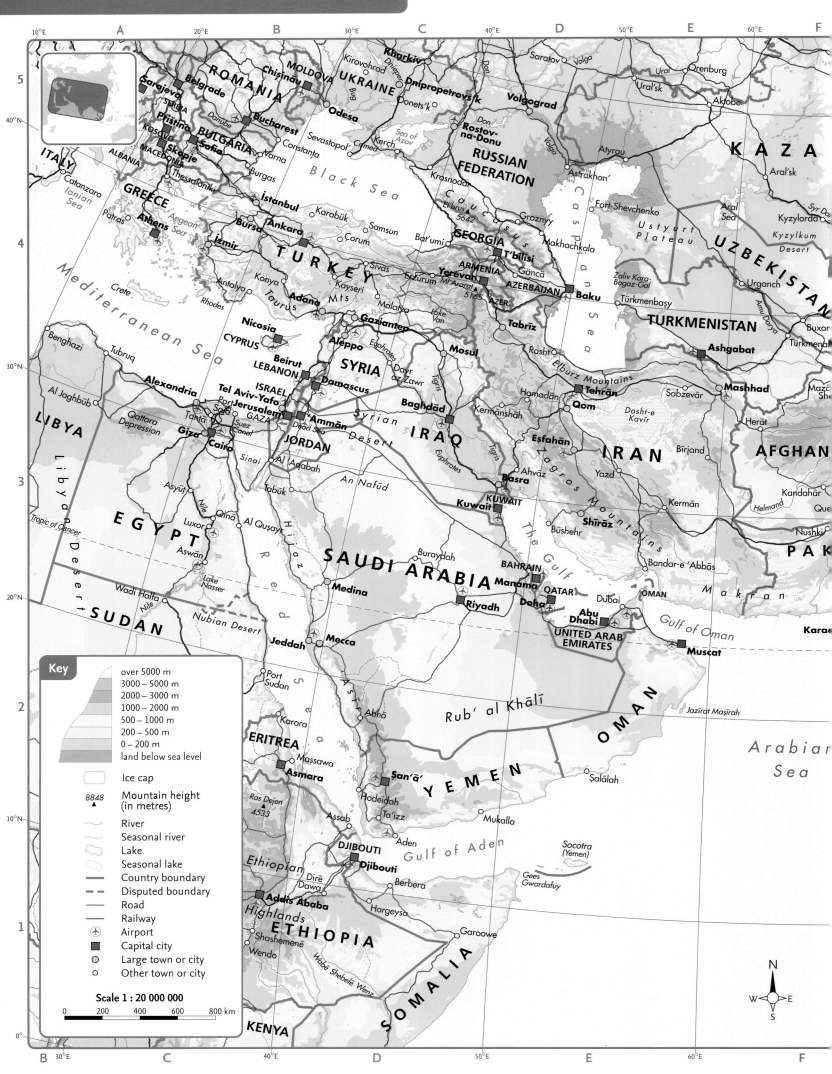

## Key

| | over 5000 m |
|---|---|
| | 3000 – 5000 m |
| | 2000 – 3000 m |
| | 1000 – 2000 m |
| | 500 – 1000 m |
| | 200 – 500 m |
| | 0 – 200 m |
| | land below sea level |

☐ Ice cap

▲ 8848 Mountain height (in metres)

River

Seasonal river

Lake

Seasonal lake

Country boundary

Disputed boundary

Road

Railway

✈ Airport

■ Capital city

● Large town or city

○ Other town or city

Scale 1 : 20 000 000

0    200    400    600    800 km

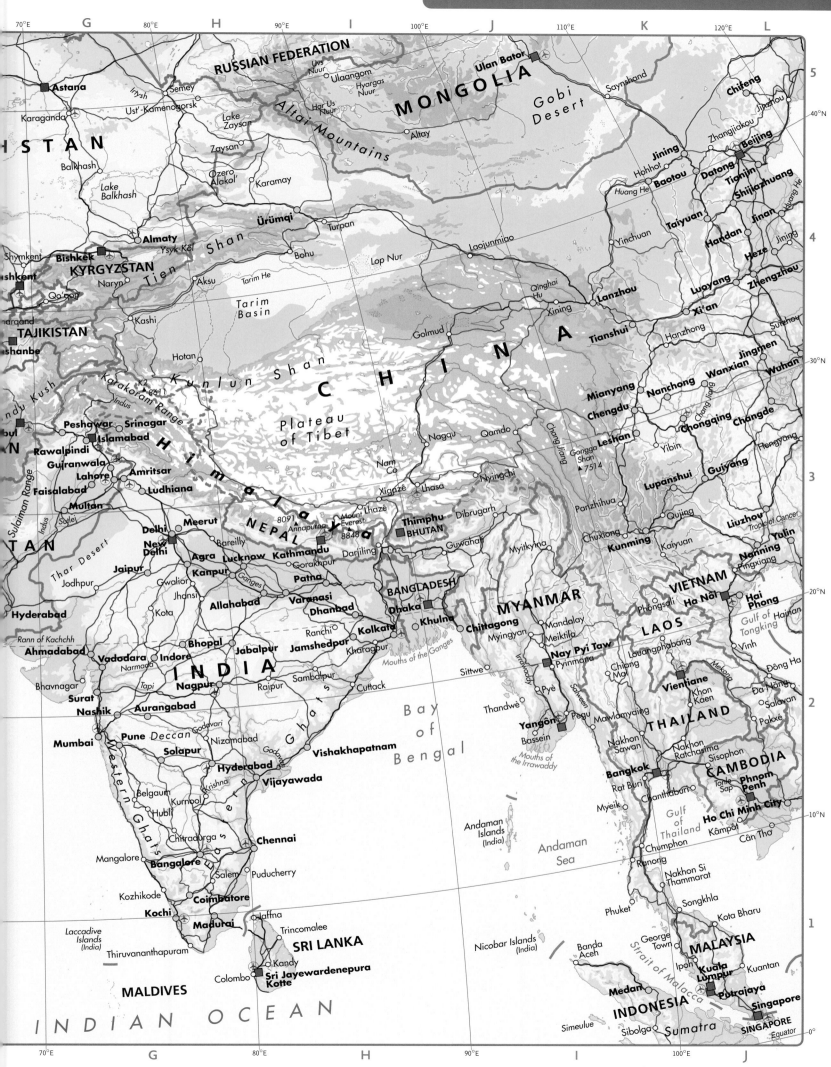

G 70°E H 80°E I 90°E J 100°E K 110°E L 120°E

RUSSIAN FEDERATION

Astana
Karaganda
Irtysh
Ust'-Kamenogorsk
Semey
Uvs Nuur
Ulaangom
Hyargas Nuur
Har Us Nuur
MONGOLIA
Gobi Desert
Ulan Bator
Saynshand
Chifeng
Jinzhou

Lake Zaysan
Zaysan
Ozero Alakol'
Karamay
Altay
Altai Mountains
Zhangjiakou
Baotou
Hohhot
Jining
Beijing
Datong
Tianjin
Shijiazhuang
Balkhash
Lake Balkhash

Shymkent
Bishkek
KYRGYZSTAN
Almaty
Ysyk-Köl
Tien Shan
Ürümqi
Turpan
Bohu
Laojunmiao
Yinchuan
Huang He
Taiyuan
Handan
Heze
Jining

shkent
Naryn
Aksu
Tarim He
Lop Nur
Qinghai Hu
Lanzhou
Luoyang
Zhengzhou

Qo'qon
Kashi
Tarim Basin
Golmud
Xining
Xi'an
Hanzhong
Suizhou

arqand
TAJIKISTAN
Hotan
Kunlun Shan
C H I N A
Tianshui
Jingmen
Wuhan

shanbe
K2 8611
Karakoram Range
Plateau of Tibet
Nagqu
Qamdo
Leshan
Gongga Shan 7514
Yibin
Chongqing
Chongde

ndu Kush
Indus
Nam Co
Xigazê
Lhasa
Nyingchi
Panzhihua
Chuxiong
Lupanshui
Guiyang

Peshawar
Srinagar
Himalaya
Mianyang
Nanchong
Chengdu

Islamabad
Rawalpindi
Gujranwala
Lahore
Amritsar
Ludhiana
8091
Annapurna
Mount Everest 8848
Thimphu
BHUTAN
Dibrugarh
Guwahati
Myitkyina
Kunming
Kaiyuan
Qujing
Liuzhou

Faisalabad
Multan
Sutlej
NEPAL
Lhazê
Darjiling
Nanning
Pingxiang
Yulin

Sulaiman Range
Delhi
Meerut
New Delhi
Agra
Lucknow
Kathmandu
Gorakhpur
Patna
Ganges
BANGLADESH
Dhaka
VIETNAM
Ha Nôi
Hai Phong

Thar Desert
Jaipur
Jodhpur
Kanpur
Gwalior
Jhansi
Allahabad
Varanasi
Dhanbad
Khulna
Chittagong
Mandalay
Myingyan
Meiktila
Phôngsali
Gulf of Tongking
Vinh

Hyderabad
Kota
Bhopal
Ranchi
Kolkata
Kharagpur
Mouths of the Ganges
MYANMAR
LAOS
Louangphabang
Đông Ha

Rann of Kachchh
Ahmadabad
Vadodara
Indore
Jabalpur
Jamshedpur
Sambalpur
Cuttack
Sittwe
Irrawaddy
Nay Pyi Taw
Pyinmana
Chiang Mai
Vientiane
Khon Kaen
Salavan
Paksé

Bhavnagar
Narmada
INDIA
Nagpur
Raipur
Pyè
THAILAND

Surat
Tapi
Godavari
Nizamabad
Thandwê
Bassein
Yangôn
Pegu
Mawlamyaing
Nakhon Sawan
Nakhon Ratchasima
Sisophon
CAMBODIA
Đà Nàng

Nashik
Aurangabad
Deccan
Vishakhapatnam
Bay of Bengal
Sittwe
Bangkok
Rat Buri
Phnom Penh
Salween

Mumbai
Pune
Solapur
Godavari
Hyderabad
Vijayawada
Mouths of the Irrawaddy
Myeik
Chanthaburi
Tonle Sap
Kâmpôt
Ho Chi Minh City
Cân Tho

Belgaum
Kurnool
Krishna
Western Ghats
Eastern Ghats
Andaman Islands (India)
Gulf of Thailand
Kâmpôt

Hubli
Chitradurga
Chennai
Andaman Sea
Chumphon
Ranong
Nakhon Si Thammarat

Mangalore
Bangalore
Salem
Puducherry
Phuket
Songkhla
Kota Bharu

Kozhikode
Coimbatore
Laccadive Islands (India)
Kochi
Madurai
Jaffna
Trincomalee
Nicobar Islands (India)
Banda Aceh
George Town
MALAYSIA
Kuantan

Thiruvananthapuram
SRI LANKA
Kandy
Ipoh
Kuala Lumpur
Strait of Malacca

MALDIVES
Colombo
Sri Jayewardenepura Kotte
Medan
Putrajaya
Singapore

I N D I A N   O C E A N
Simeulue
Sibolga
Sumatra
INDONESIA
SINGAPORE
Equator

Lambert Azimuthal Equal Area projection

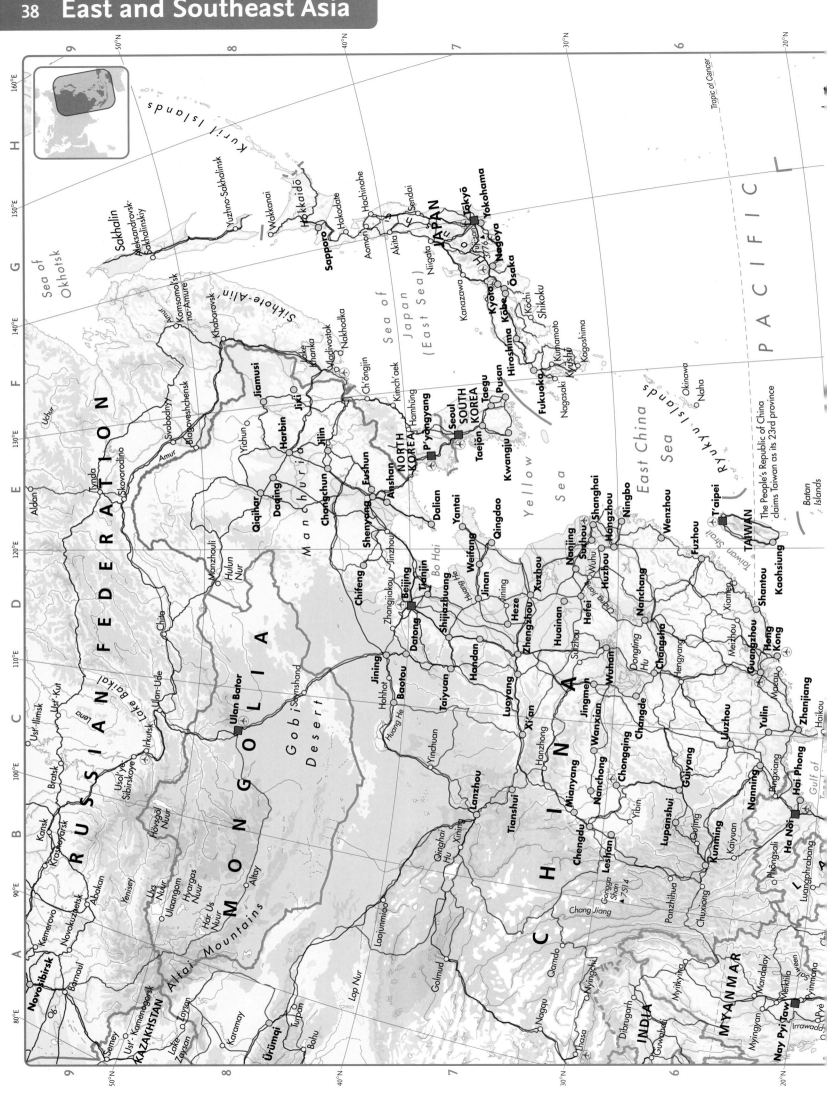

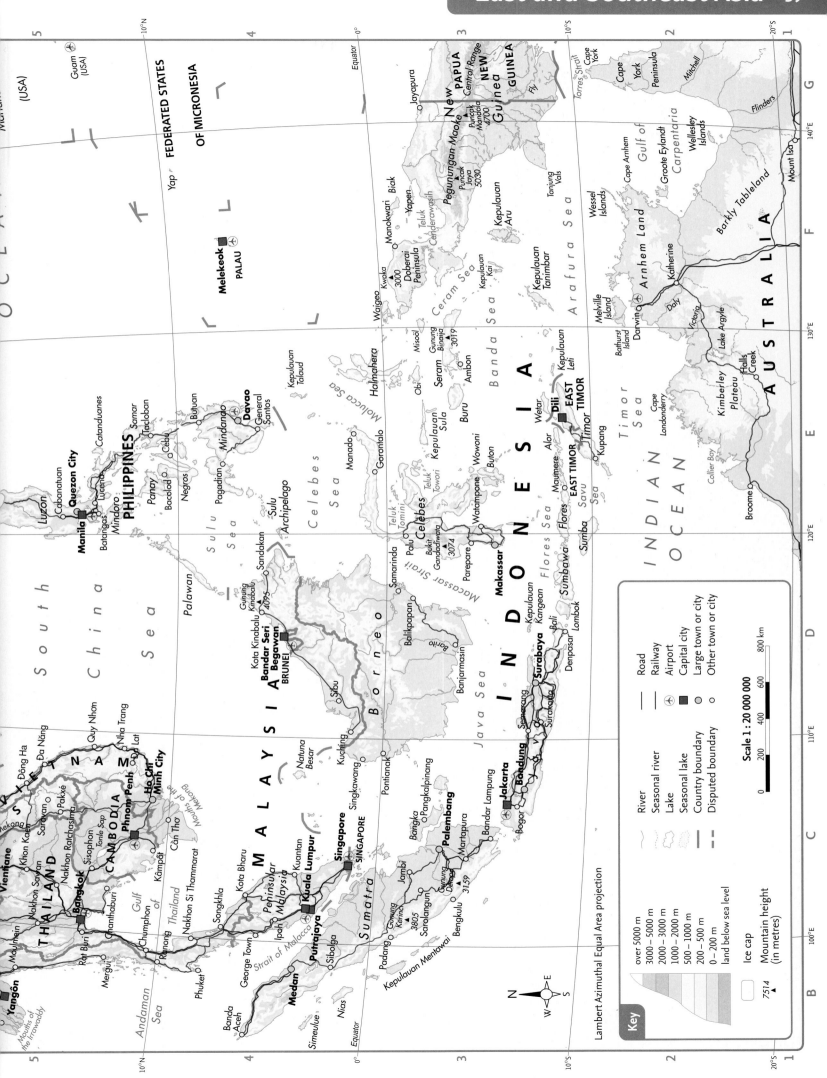

Key

over 5000 m
3000 – 5000 m
2000 – 3000 m
1000 – 2000 m
500 – 1000 m
200 – 500 m
0 – 200 m
land below sea level

Ice cap

7514 ▲ Mountain height (in metres)

| | | Road |
| | | Railway |
| | ✈ | Airport |
| | ■ | Capital city |
| | ● | Large town or city |
| | ○ | Other town or city |

— River
〰 Seasonal river
Lake
Seasonal lake
— Country boundary
- - Disputed boundary

Scale 1 : 20 000 000

0   200   400   600   800 km

Lambert Azimuthal Equal Area projection

N
W   E
S

**Facts about Japan**

**Landscape**
Area: 377 727 sq km
Highest point: Fuji-san 3776 m

**Population**
Total: 127 156 000
Density: 337 persons per sq km

**Settlement**
% Urban population: 66
Main towns: Tōkyō, Ōsaka-Kōbe,
Nagoya, Fukuoka-Kita-Kyūshū

**Land use**
Main crops: Rice, potatoes, sugar beets
Main industries: Electrical equipment,
transport equipment, other machinery,
chemicals

**Development indicators**
Life expectancy: male 79, female 86
GNI per capita: US$ 37 790
Primary school enrolment ratio: 100
% Access to safe water: 100

**Key**

3000 – 5000 m
2000 – 3000 m
1000 – 2000 m
500 – 1000 m
200 – 500 m
0 – 200 m

3776 ▲ Mountain height
(in metres)

River
Lake

—— Country boundary
– – – Disputed boundary
—— Road
—— Railway
········ Ferry
✈ Airport
■ Capital city
⊙ Large town or city
○ Other town or city

**Japanese name forms**

-dake          peak
-hanto         peninsula
-jima          island
-kai           bay, inlet
-kaikyo        strait
-ko            lake
-nada          sea, gulf
-retto         chain of islands
-san           mountain
-sanchi        mountainous area
-shima         island
-suido         strait, channel
-to            island
-wan           sea
-yama          mountain

Scale 1 : 7 500 000

0    100    200    300    400 km

N
W    E
S

Albers Equal Area Conic projection

## Annual rainfall

The driest parts of Japan are in the north, on the island of Hokkaidō. Most rain falls on the high mountain tops and the southern and western coasts.

**Average annual rainfall**

- more than 3000 mm
- 2000 – 3000 mm
- 1500 – 2000 mm
- 1000 – 1500 mm
- less than 1000 mm

**Scale 1 : 15 000 000**

? What affects Japan's climate?

## Climate statistics

The tables below list average monthly temperature in degrees centigrade and average monthly rainfall in millimetres for three weather stations in Japan.

Tōkyō

| Sapporo | Jan | Feb | Mar | Apr | May | Jun | Jul | Aug | Sep | Oct | Nov | Dec |
|---|---|---|---|---|---|---|---|---|---|---|---|---|
| Temperature - °C | -5 | -4 | 0 | 6 | 12 | 16 | 20 | 21 | 17 | 11 | 4 | -2 |
| Rainfall - mm | 114 | 92 | 78 | 65 | 59 | 76 | 80 | 131 | 142 | 115 | 104 | 101 |

| Tōkyō | Jan | Feb | Mar | Apr | May | Jun | Jul | Aug | Sep | Oct | Nov | Dec |
|---|---|---|---|---|---|---|---|---|---|---|---|---|
| Temperature - °C | 5 | 5 | 8 | 14 | 18 | 22 | 25 | 27 | 23 | 17 | 12 | 7 |
| Rainfall - mm | 54 | 63 | 102 | 128 | 148 | 181 | 125 | 137 | 193 | 181 | 93 | 56 |

| Kagoshima | Jan | Feb | Mar | Apr | May | Jun | Jul | Aug | Sep | Oct | Nov | Dec |
|---|---|---|---|---|---|---|---|---|---|---|---|---|
| Temperature - °C | 7 | 8 | 11 | 16 | 20 | 23 | 27 | 28 | 25 | 20 | 14 | 9 |
| Rainfall - mm | 95 | 106 | 147 | 256 | 275 | 475 | 323 | 209 | 211 | 108 | 92 | 80 |

## Temperature: January

In January temperatures fall below 0°C in the north of Japan. On the south coast and on the southern island of Kyūshū the winter is much milder.

**Average temperature**

- 4 – 8°C
- 0 – 4°C
- -8 – 0°C
- below -8°C

→ Wind direction

**Scale 1 : 15 000 000**

## Temperature: August

Most of Japan is very warm during the summer, especially in the southern part of the country. Temperatures are cooler on the high mountains in the north.

**Average temperature**

- over 26°C
- 22 – 26°C
- 18 – 22°C
- below 18°C

→ Wind direction

**Scale 1 : 15 000 000**

WWW Japan Meteorological Agency
www.jma.go.jp
World Meteorological Organization
www.wmo.ch

Japan is situated on the 'Ring of Fire' around the Pacific Ocean. There are almost 200 volcanoes in the 'Ring of Fire' and over 20 are still active.

Earthquakes are more disastrous than volcanic eruptions in Japan where 5000 earthquakes are recorded annually. The main earthquake zones lie on the Pacific side of Japan. Strong earthquakes may destroy roads and railways, collapse houses and result in many casualties.

**Earthquake seismogram :**
A seismogram is used to record the horizontal or vertical vibration caused during the course of an earthquake. The vertical divisions represent time intervals of 5 seconds.

## Volcanic activity

Volcanic zones

Plate boundary

Eurasian Plate

Japan Trench

Nankai Trench

Pacific Plate

Philippine Plate

*Where do volcanoes and earthquakes occur?*

Volcanic rocks

▲ Active volcano (erupted since 1850)

△ Other volcano

● Major earthquake

**Scale 1 : 9 000 000**

**Kōbe earthquake :**
In 1995 Kōbe was struck by a huge earthquake which measured 7.1 on the Richter Scale. The centre of the quake was close to the city, caused extensive damage and killed over 5000 people.

Tokachi

*Hokkaidō*

Sapporo

Usu

*Komaga-take*

*Chokai*

*Zao*

*Honshū*

*Yake-Dake*

Tōkyō

*Fuji*

Nagoya

Kōbe

*Shikoku*

*Unzen* △ Aso

*Kyūshū*

Kagoshima ▲ *Kirishima*

▲ *Sakurajima*

**Fuji :**
Situated on the island of Honshū, Fuji is a dormant volcano which has not erupted since 1707. At 3776 m, it is the highest mountain in Japan and has a crater which is 610 metres in diameter.

## Richter Scale

The scale of measurement used to describe the strength of an earthquake is known as the Richter Scale. The scale measures the energy which is released at the centre of an earthquake. Every year about 50 000 quakes measuring 3 – 4 are recorded worldwide, while only 800 measuring 5 – 6 occur.

Over 8.0 most powerful earthquake

7.0 – 8.0 major earthquake

6.0 – 7.0 destructive earthquake

4.5 – 6.0 earthquake causes local damage

3.5 – 4.5 earthquake felt by many people

2.5 – 3.5 earthquake recorded but not felt

below 2.5 earthquake not recorded

**Sakurajima :**
Sakurajima is an active volcano situated in Kagoshima Bay. Its eruptions are generally gentle with little explosive activity.

WWW **USGS National Earthquake Information Center**
earthquake.usgs.gov/regional/neic
**Earthquake Research Institute**
www.eri.u-tokyo.ac.jp

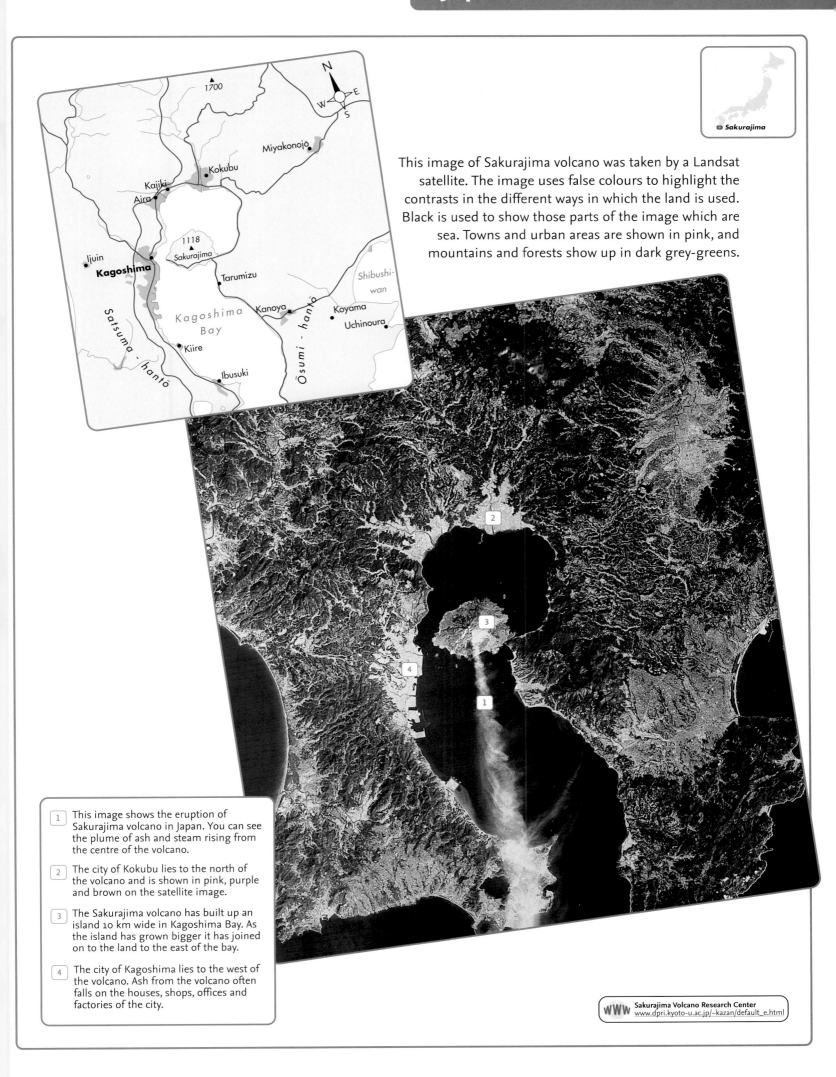

This image of Sakurajima volcano was taken by a Landsat satellite. The image uses false colours to highlight the contrasts in the different ways in which the land is used. Black is used to show those parts of the image which are sea. Towns and urban areas are shown in pink, and mountains and forests show up in dark grey-greens.

1 This image shows the eruption of Sakurajima volcano in Japan. You can see the plume of ash and steam rising from the centre of the volcano.

2 The city of Kokubu lies to the north of the volcano and is shown in pink, purple and brown on the satellite image.

3 The Sakurajima volcano has built up an island 10 km wide in Kagoshima Bay. As the island has grown bigger it has joined on to the land to the east of the bay.

4 The city of Kagoshima lies to the west of the volcano. Ash from the volcano often falls on the houses, shops, offices and factories of the city.

www Sakurajima Volcano Research Center
www.dpri.kyoto-u.ac.jp/~kazan/default_e.html

## Landscape

The landscape of China ranges from high mountains and plateaux in the west to lower plains in the east. Its major rivers flow from west to east towards the Pacific Ocean.

### Facts about China

**Landscape**
Area: 9 584 492 sq km
Highest point: Gongga Shan 7514 m

**Population**
Total: 1 330 265 000
Density: 139 persons per sq km

**Settlement**
% Urban population: 42
Main towns/cities: Beijing, Shanghai, Wuhan, Guangzhou, Shenzhen

**Land use**
Main crops: Rice, wheat, potatoes, corn, peanuts
Main industries: Electrical and other machinery, clothing, textiles, iron and steel

**Development indicators**
Life expectancy: male 71, female 75
GNI per capita: US$ 2370
Primary school enrolment ratio: 99
% Access to safe water: 88

## Earthquake zones

China is located in one of the most active seismic regions of the world. In the Tangshan earthquake, in 1976, over 240 000 people lost their lives and more recently, in 2008, 80 000 people were killed during the earthquake in Sichuan Province.

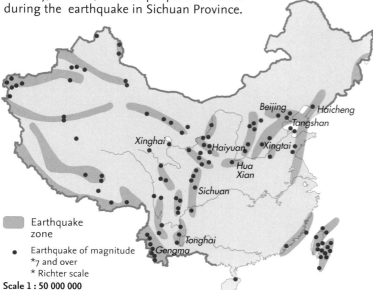

Earthquake zone

• Earthquake of magnitude *7 and over
  * Richter scale

Scale 1 : 50 000 000

## Population

China has been the world's most populous nation for many centuries. In the early 1970s, the government implemented a stringent one-child birth-control policy in an attempt to slow down the population growth rate which is now more stable. Life expectancy has risen and China has an increasingly ageing population.

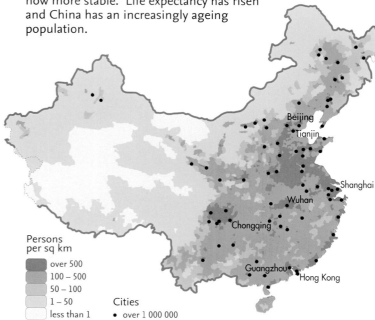

**Persons per sq km**

over 500
100 – 500
50 – 100
1 – 50
less than 1

Cities
• over 1 000 000

Scale 1 : 50 000 000

## Population change

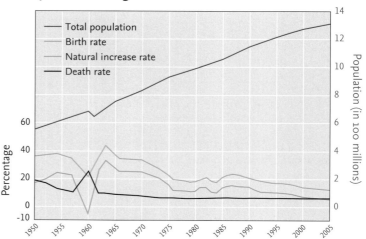

- Total population
- Birth rate
- Natural increase rate
- Death rate

## Population structure

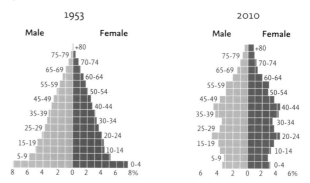

Each full square represents 1% of the total population

## Environmental pollution

Rapid industrial development and an increase in energy consumption in China has resulted in serious pollution problems such as smog and degradation of natural resources.

Many of the world's most polluted cities are in China. Acid rain falls on nearly one third of the country.

## Soil degradation and desertification

Almost all of China's rivers are polluted to some degree. Overgrazing and the expansion of agricultural land has led to serious desertification in northern China.

Plans to combat these problems include forest planting schemes, pollution control projects and the installation of rubbish treatment plants.

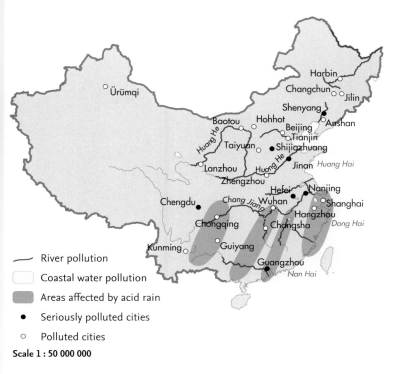

River pollution

Coastal water pollution

Areas affected by acid rain

● Seriously polluted cities

○ Polluted cities

**Scale 1 : 50 000 000**

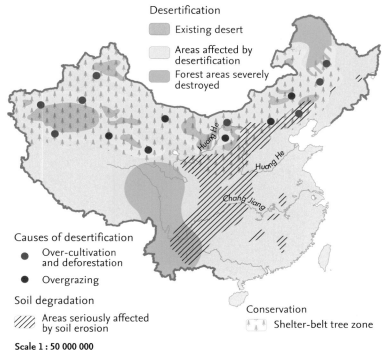

Desertification

Existing desert

Areas affected by desertification

Forest areas severely destroyed

Causes of desertification

● Over-cultivation and deforestation

● Overgrazing

Soil degradation

/// Areas seriously affected by soil erosion

Conservation

Shelter-belt tree zone

**Scale 1 : 50 000 000**

## Three Gorges Dam

The Three Gorges Dam, spanning the Chang Jiang in China, is the largest hydroelectric power project in the world. The dam body was completed in 2006 and the length of the reservoir is 600 kilometres. The project produces clean electricity, prevents deadly floods downstream and improves navigation.

The dam has also flooded archaeological and cultural sites and displaced some 1.24 million people and is causing dramatic ecological changes.

? What is the cost of rapid economic growth?

Area affected by Three Gorges project

Area inundated

Three Gorges Dam

Provincial boundary

▼ Gorge

● Inundated town

**Scale 1 : 4 500 000**

An aerial view of the Three Gorges Dam with the dam clearly visible in the bottom right hand corner.

Space Imaging

WWW USGS National Earthquake Information Center
www.earthquake.usgs.gov/regional/neic
International Rivers
www.internationalrivers.org
China Population Information and Research Center    www.un.org/Depts/escap/pop/china/welcome.htm

**Facts about Africa**

**Area**
30 343 578 sq km

**Highest peak**
Kilimanjaro 5892 m

**Lowest point**
Lake Assal -156 m

**Longest river**
Nile 6695 km

**Largest lake**
Lake Victoria 68 800 sq km

**Key**

over 5000 m
3000 – 5000 m
2000 – 3000 m
1000 – 2000 m
500 – 1000 m
200 – 500 m
0 – 200 m
land below sea level

5892 ▲ Mountain height (in metres)

**Scale 1 : 37 000 000**

0    500    1000    1500 km

Lambert Azimuthal Equal Area projection

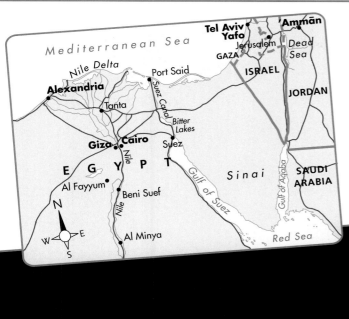

This is an infra-red satellite image of the delta of the river Nile, the Sinai peninsula and the neighbouring parts of Israel, Jordan and Saudi Arabia. Most of this area is desert and this is shown in the pale pinky-brown colour. The red colour in the delta of the river Nile shows that most of the land here is used for farming. The pale blue areas on the edge of the delta are shallow lagoons.

Connections - Africa and Asia.

1  The city of Cairo is the dark grey area at the base of the delta.

2  The valley of the river Nile is shown as a dark line which ends at the delta.

3  The Suez Canal was built in 1869 by connecting a series of lakes which are shown in black. The Suez Canal allows ships to sail from the Mediterranean Sea, in the north of the image, to the Red Sea.

4  The Red Sea is shown in black on the image. The pale grey areas in the sea are islands.

5  The Dead Sea in Israel is shown in black on the satellite image.

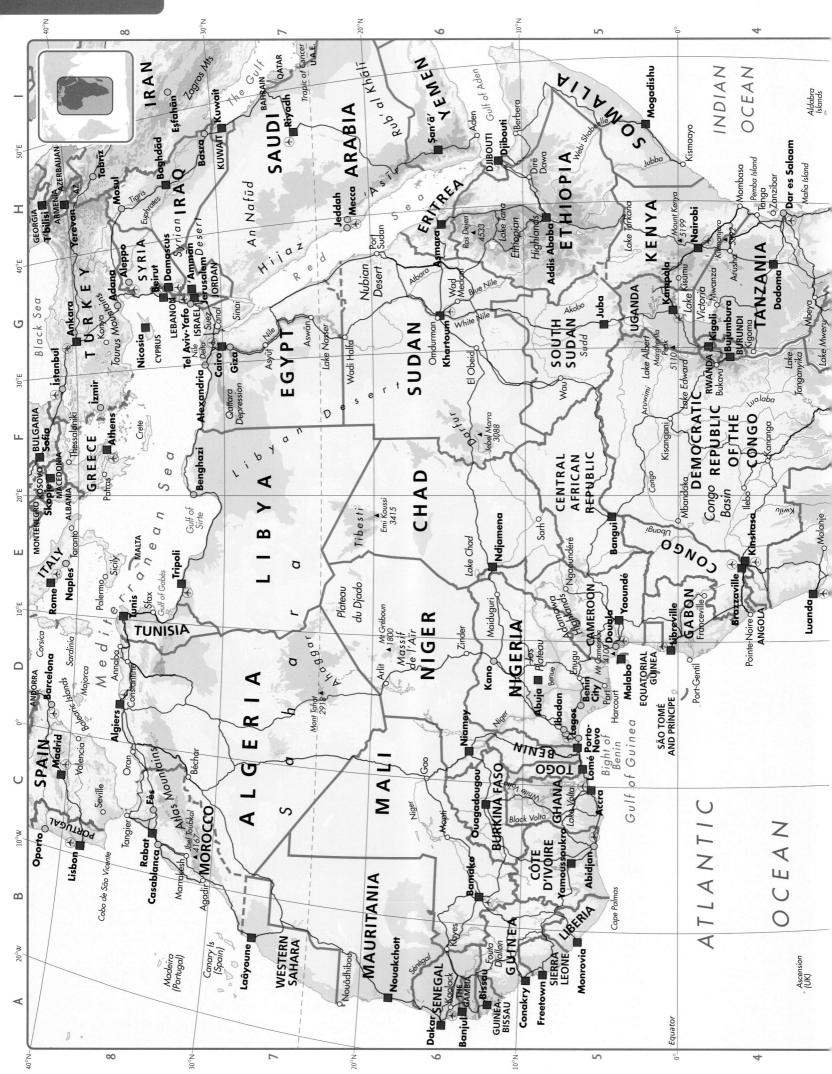

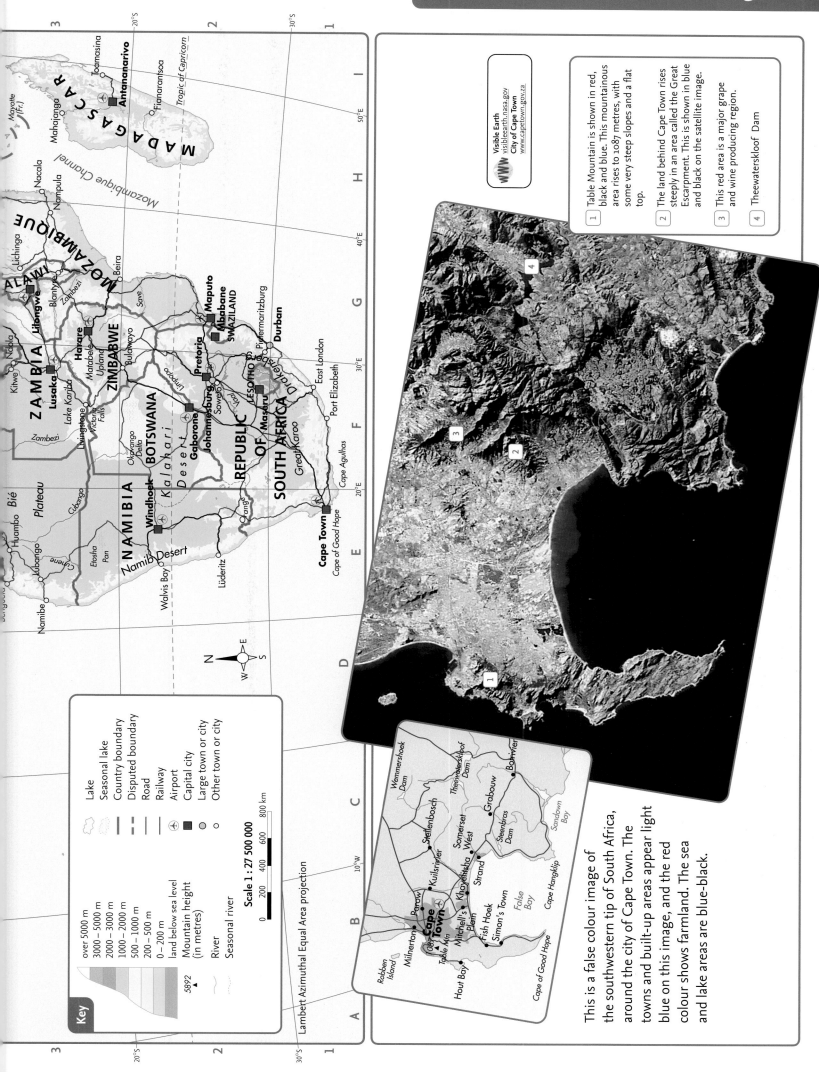

**Visible Earth**
visibleearth.nasa.gov
**City of Cape Town**
www.capetown.gov.za

1  Table Mountain is shown in red, black and blue. This mountainous area rises to 1087 metres, with some very steep slopes and a flat top.

2  The land behind Cape Town rises steeply in an area called the Great Escarpment. This is shown in blue and black on the satellite image.

3  This red area is a major grape and wine producing region.

4  Theewaterskloof Dam

This is a false colour image of the southwestern tip of South Africa, around the city of Cape Town. The towns and built-up areas appear light blue on this image, and the red colour shows farmland. The sea and lake areas are blue-black.

## Key

Lake
Seasonal lake
Country boundary
Disputed boundary
Road
Railway
Airport
Capital city
Large town or city
Other town or city

over 5000 m
3000–5000 m
2000–3000 m
1000–2000 m
500–1000 m
200–500 m
0–200 m
land below sea level

Mountain height (in metres)

5892 ▲

River
Seasonal river

Scale 1 : 27 500 000

0   200   400   600   800 km

Lambert Azimuthal Equal Area projection

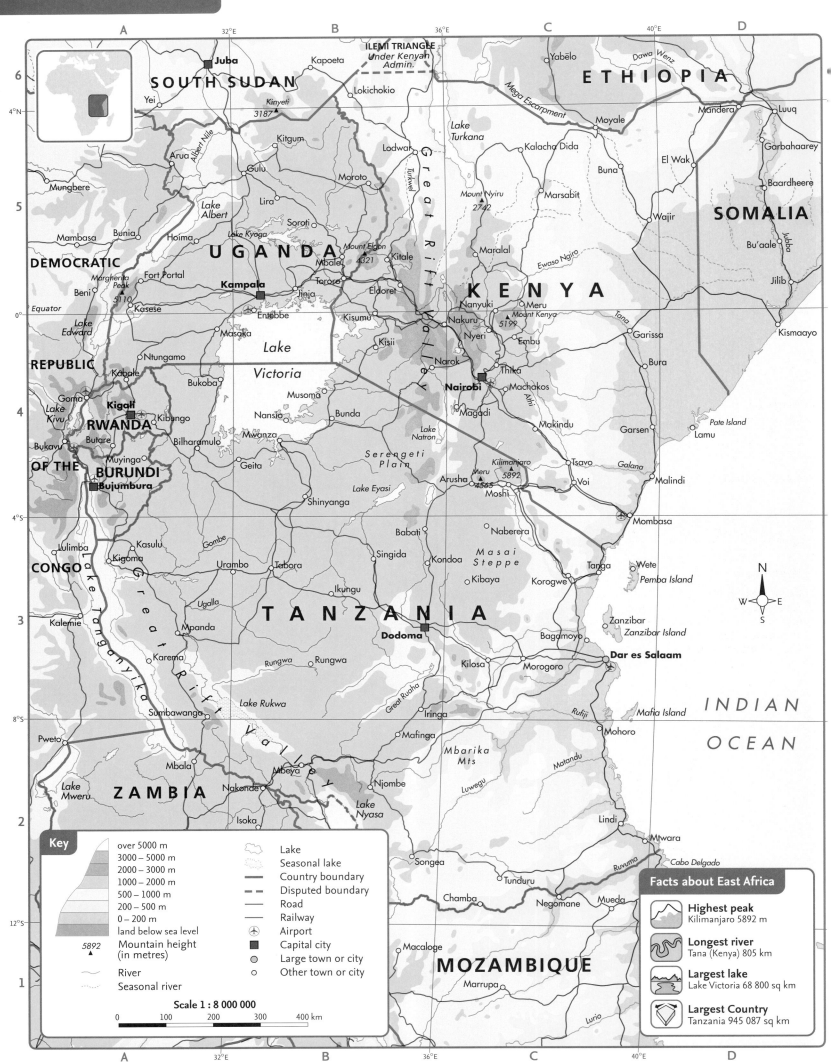

**Key**

| | |
|---|---|
| over 5000 m | |
| 3000 – 5000 m | |
| 2000 – 3000 m | |
| 1000 – 2000 m | |
| 500 – 1000 m | |
| 200 – 500 m | |
| 0 – 200 m | |
| land below sea level | |

▲5892  Mountain height (in metres)

～  River
‥‥‥  Seasonal river

| | |
|---|---|
| | Lake |
| | Seasonal lake |
| —— | Country boundary |
| - - - | Disputed boundary |
| —— | Road |
| —— | Railway |
| ✈ | Airport |
| ■ | Capital city |
| ● | Large town or city |
| ○ | Other town or city |

Scale 1 : 8 000 000

0    100    200    300    400 km

**Facts about East Africa**

**Highest peak**
Kilimanjaro 5892 m

**Longest river**
Tana (Kenya) 805 km

**Largest lake**
Lake Victoria 68 800 sq km

**Largest Country**
Tanzania 945 087 sq km

Lambert Azimuthal Equal Area projection

## Annual rainfall

The heaviest rain falls in April and May. The highlands and western areas receive ample rainfall but most of the north and northeast is very dry.

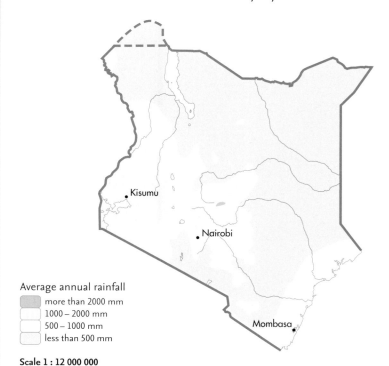

Average annual rainfall

more than 2000 mm
1000 – 2000 mm
500 – 1000 mm
less than 500 mm

Scale 1 : 12 000 000

 What can we find out about Kenya?

## Climate statistics

Kenya has a tropical climate which varies with altitude. The coastal lowland area is hot and humid but the highlands region is much drier and cooler.

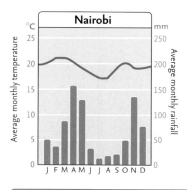

WWW National Bureau of Statistics
www.knbs.or.ke
Met Office Africa Weather
www.metoffice.gov.uk/weather

| Nairobi | Jan | Feb | Mar | Apr | May | Jun | Jul | Aug | Sep | Oct | Nov | Dec |
|---|---|---|---|---|---|---|---|---|---|---|---|---|
| Temperature - °C | 20 | 21 | 21 | 20 | 19 | 18 | 17 | 17 | 19 | 20 | 19 | 19 |
| Rainfall - mm | 49 | 36 | 85 | 153 | 126 | 32 | 13 | 18 | 21 | 48 | 132 | 75 |

| Mombasa | Jan | Feb | Mar | Apr | May | Jun | Jul | Aug | Sep | Oct | Nov | Dec |
|---|---|---|---|---|---|---|---|---|---|---|---|---|
| Temperature - °C | 28 | 28 | 28 | 28 | 26 | 25 | 24 | 24 | 25 | 26 | 27 | 28 |
| Rainfall - mm | 17 | 10 | 30 | 108 | 149 | 54 | 34 | 47 | 46 | 62 | 66 | 32 |

| Kisumu | Jan | Feb | Mar | Apr | May | Jun | Jul | Aug | Sep | Oct | Nov | Dec |
|---|---|---|---|---|---|---|---|---|---|---|---|---|
| Temperature - °C | 24 | 24 | 24 | 23 | 23 | 22 | 22 | 22 | 23 | 24 | 24 | 23 |
| Rainfall - mm | 62 | 88 | 163 | 207 | 173 | 93 | 63 | 90 | 82 | 72 | 111 | 107 |

## Vegetation

Large areas of Kenya are covered in sparsely wooded Savanna. The most varied vegetation is found in the highlands where Savanna gives way to woodland and forest. North of the river Tana semi desert areas support little vegetation.

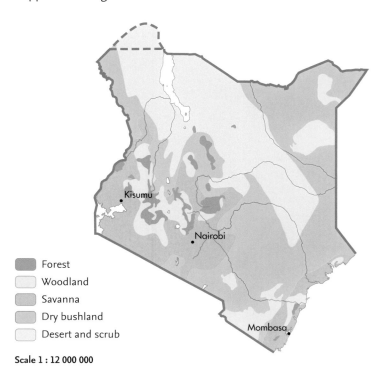

Forest
Woodland
Savanna
Dry bushland
Desert and scrub

Scale 1 : 12 000 000

## Population

Kenya's population is distributed very unevenly. The most densely populated areas are found in areas with adequate rainfall. The main urban settlements are Nairobi and Mombasa. The dry north and northeast areas are sparsely populated as lack of water limits the development of any settlement.

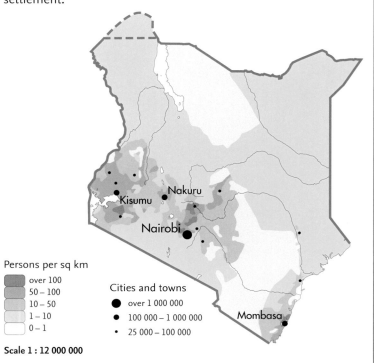

Persons per sq km

over 100
50 – 100
10 – 50
1 – 10
0 – 1

Cities and towns

over 1 000 000
100 000 – 1 000 000
25 000 – 100 000

Scale 1 : 12 000 000

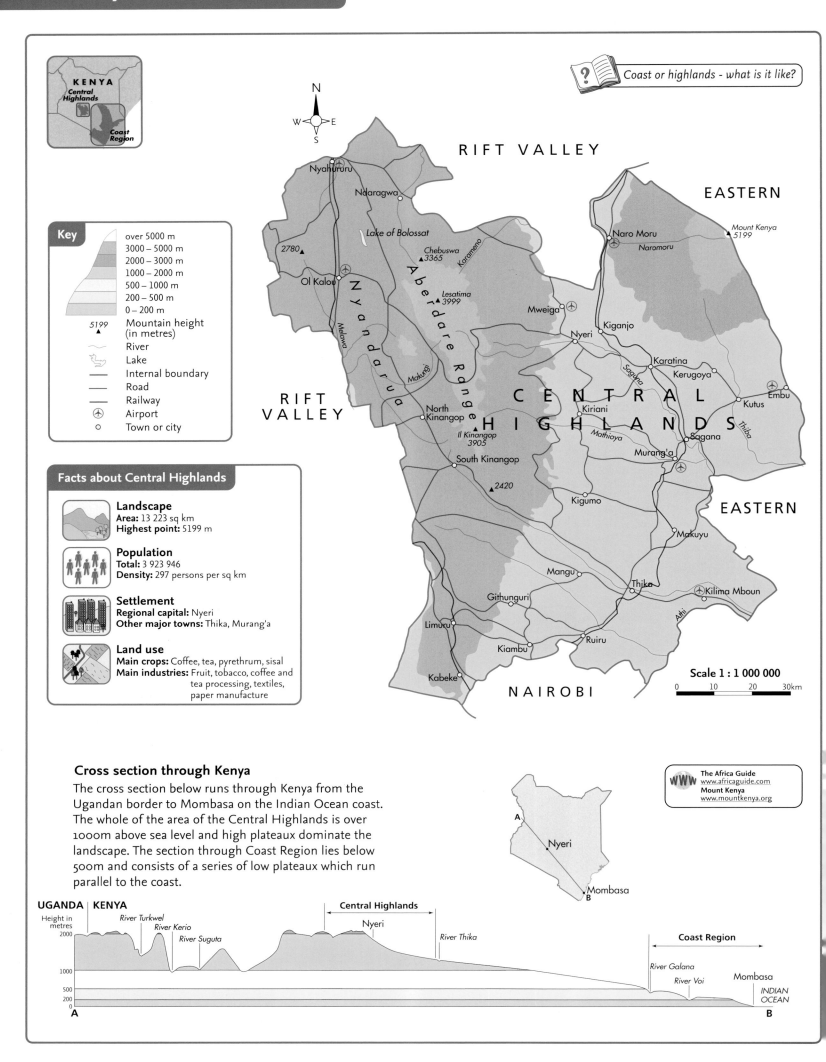

**KENYA**
Central Highlands

Coast Region

Coast or highlands - what is it like?

**RIFT VALLEY**

**EASTERN**

N
W　　E
S

## Key

| | |
|---|---|
| | over 5000 m |
| | 3000 – 5000 m |
| | 2000 – 3000 m |
| | 1000 – 2000 m |
| | 500 – 1000 m |
| | 200 – 500 m |
| | 0 – 200 m |
| 5199 ▲ | Mountain height (in metres) |
| | River |
| | Lake |
| | Internal boundary |
| | Road |
| | Railway |
| ✈ | Airport |
| ○ | Town or city |

Nyahururu

Ndaragwa

Lake of Bolossat

2780 ▲

Chebuswa ▲3365

Karameno

Naro Moru

Mount Kenya ▲5199

Naromoru

Ol Kalou

Lesatima ▲3999

Mweiga

Nyeri

Kiganjo

Melawa

Nyandarua

Makungi

Aberdare Range

Sagana

Karatina

Kerugoya

**CENTRAL**

Embu

**HIGHLANDS**

North Kinangop

Il Kinangop 3905

Kiriani

Mathioya

Kutus

Thiba

## Facts about Central Highlands

### Landscape
**Area:** 13 223 sq km
**Highest point:** 5199 m

### Population
**Total:** 3 923 946
**Density:** 297 persons per sq km

### Settlement
**Regional capital:** Nyeri
**Other major towns:** Thika, Murang'a

### Land use
**Main crops:** Coffee, tea, pyrethrum, sisal
**Main industries:** Fruit, tobacco, coffee and tea processing, textiles, paper manufacture

South Kinangop

2420

Kigumo

Murang'a

Sagana

Makuyu

**EASTERN**

Mangu

Thika

Kilima Mboun

Githunguri

Athi

Limuru

Ruiru

Kiambu

Kabeke

**NAIROBI**

Scale 1 : 1 000 000

0　10　20　30km

## Cross section through Kenya

The cross section below runs through Kenya from the Ugandan border to Mombasa on the Indian Ocean coast. The whole of the area of the Central Highlands is over 1000m above sea level and high plateaux dominate the landscape. The section through Coast Region lies below 500m and consists of a series of low plateaux which run parallel to the coast.

A
Nyeri
Mombasa
B

**The Africa Guide**
www.africaguide.com
**Mount Kenya**
www.mountkenya.org

**UGANDA** | **KENYA**

Height in metres

Central Highlands

River Turkwel
Nyeri

River Kerio

River Suguta

River Thika

**Coast Region**

2000

1000

River Galana

River Voi

Mombasa

500
200

**INDIAN OCEAN**

A　　　　　　　　　　　　　　　　　　　　　　　B

Modified Polyconic projection

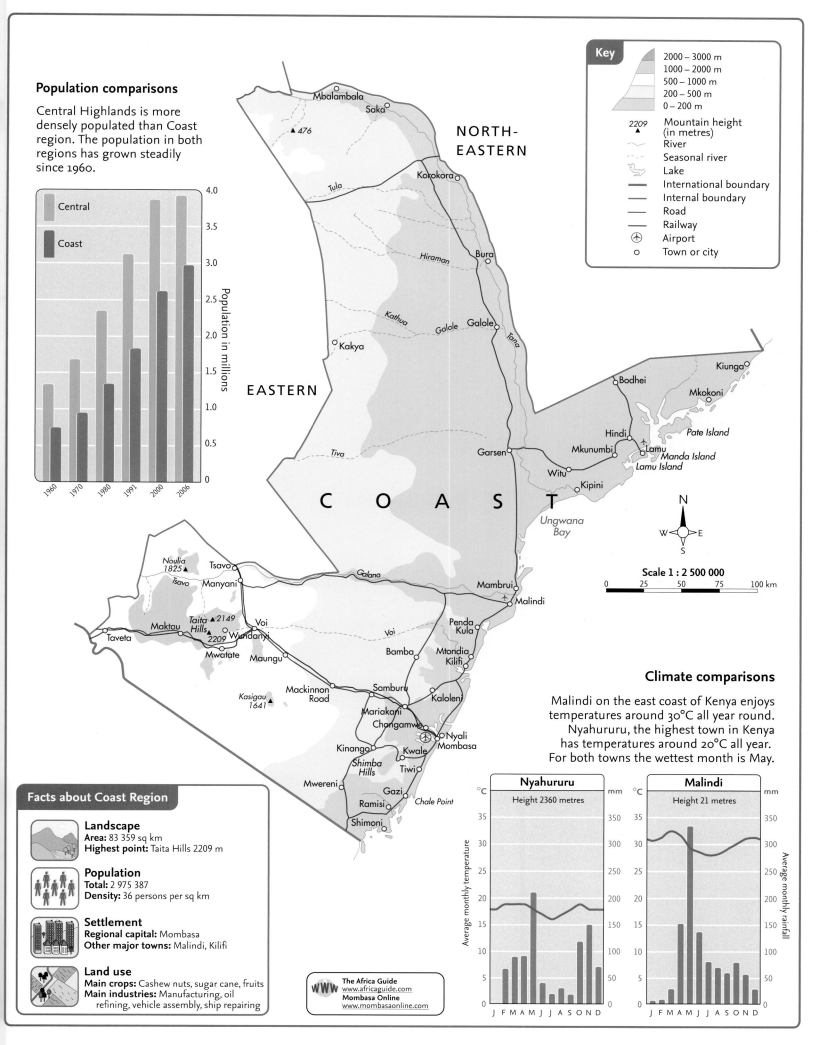

## Population comparisons

Central Highlands is more densely populated than Coast region. The population in both regions has grown steadily since 1960.

Central
Coast

Population in millions

4.0
3.5
3.0
2.5
2.0
1.5
1.0
0.5
0

1960 1970 1980 1991 2000 2006

### Key

2000 – 3000 m
1000 – 2000 m
500 – 1000 m
200 – 500 m
0 – 200 m

2209 ▲ Mountain height (in metres)
River
Seasonal river
Lake
International boundary
Internal boundary
Road
Railway
✈ Airport
○ Town or city

NORTH-EASTERN

EASTERN

COAST

Mbalambala
Saka
▲ 476
Tula
Korokora
Hiraman
Bura
Kathua
Galole  Galole
Tana
Kakya
Tiva
Garsen
Witu
Kipini
Ungwana Bay
Kiunga
Bodhei
Mkokoni
Hindi
Mkunumbi  Lamu
Pate Island
Manda Island
Lamu Island

N
W  E
S

Scale 1 : 2 500 000

0  25  50  75  100 km

Noulia 1825 ▲  Tsavo
Tsavo
Manyani
Galana
Mambrui
Malindi
Maktau  Taita ▲ 2149
Hills ▲ 2209
Wundanyi
Taveta
Mwatate  Maungu
Voi
Penda Kula
Bamba
Mtondia Kilifi
Kasigau 1641 ▲
Mackinnon Road
Samburu
Kaloleni
Mariakani
Changamwe
Kinango  Nyali Mombasa
Kwale
Shimba Hills  Tiwi
Mwereni
Gazi
Ramisi  Chale Point
Shimoni

### Climate comparisons

Malindi on the east coast of Kenya enjoys temperatures around 30°C all year round. Nyahururu, the highest town in Kenya has temperatures around 20°C all year. For both towns the wettest month is May.

| Nyahururu | | Malindi | |
|---|---|---|---|
| °C | mm | °C | mm |

Height 2360 metres

Height 21 metres

Average monthly temperature
Average monthly rainfall

35  350
30  300
25  250
20  200
15  150
10  100
5  50
0  0

J F M A M J J A S O N D

J F M A M J J A S O N D

### Facts about Coast Region

**Landscape**
Area: 83 359 sq km
Highest point: Taita Hills 2209 m

**Population**
Total: 2 975 387
Density: 36 persons per sq km

**Settlement**
Regional capital: Mombasa
Other major towns: Malindi, Kilifi

**Land use**
Main crops: Cashew nuts, sugar cane, fruits
Main industries: Manufacturing, oil refining, vehicle assembly, ship repairing

www  The Africa Guide
www.africaguide.com
Mombasa Online
www.mombasaonline.com

Modified Polyconic projection

## Tourism

Tourism makes an important contribution to Kenya's economy. The main attractions are wildlife in the National Parks and National Reserves, and the resorts on the Indian Ocean coast. The temperature is over 20°C throughout the country all year.

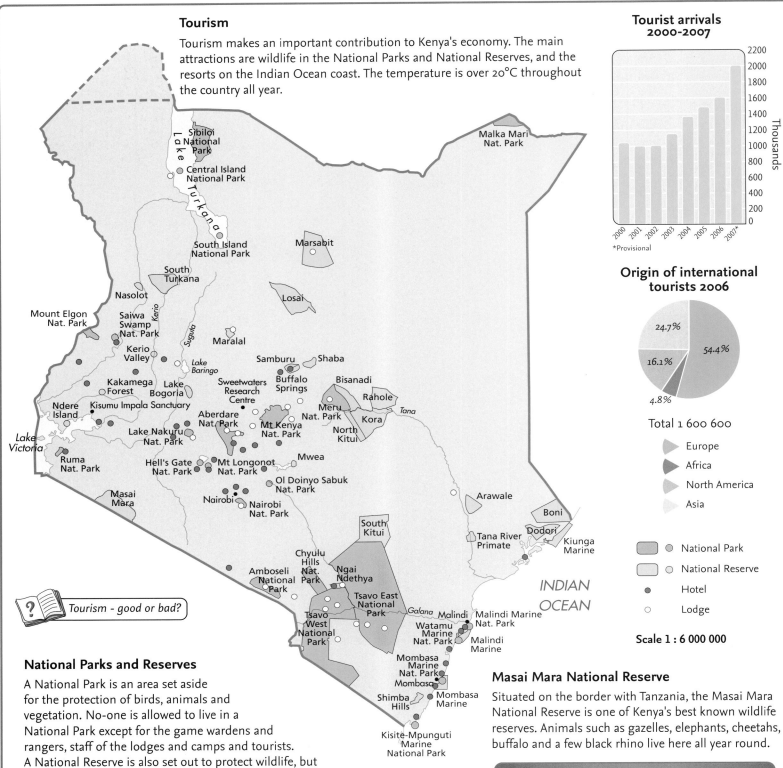

### Tourist arrivals
**2000-2007**

*Provisional

### Origin of international tourists 2006

24.7%
54.4%
16.1%
4.8%

Total 1 600 600

Europe
Africa
North America
Asia

National Park
National Reserve
Hotel
Lodge

Scale 1 : 6 000 000

*Tourism - good or bad?*

## National Parks and Reserves

A National Park is an area set aside for the protection of birds, animals and vegetation. No-one is allowed to live in a National Park except for the game wardens and rangers, staff of the lodges and camps and tourists. A National Reserve is also set out to protect wildlife, but local people can live and keep their cattle in the reserve.

## Masai Mara National Reserve

Situated on the border with Tanzania, the Masai Mara National Reserve is one of Kenya's best known wildlife reserves. Animals such as gazelles, elephants, cheetahs, buffalo and a few black rhino live here all year round.

## Endangered species - Rhinos

Since 1980 the Rhino population has declined, due mainly to hunting. Sanctuaries such as the Sweetwaters Research Centre are dedicated to the conservation of the Black Rhino. By 2010 the aim is to increase the population to 650.

### Black Rhino population

| 1980 | 1987 | 1993 | 2003 | 2005 |
|------|------|------|------|------|
| 1500 | 521  | 417  | 428  | 539  |

For four months every year herds of wildebeest from Tanzania graze on the Mara plains. Tall grasses are reduced to stubble before the herds trek south again.

Threats to the natural environment in East Africa include deforestation, soil erosion, desertification, water shortage and water pollution. Forest output has declined due to over exploitation and soil erosion has resulted in the silting of dams and the loss of biodiversity.

The three case studies below outline some of the current environmental problems faced in East African countries.

In the 1970's, the Green Belt Movement founded by Maathai Wangari, focused on the planting of trees and environmental conservation. Over the years 30 million seedling trees have been planted in an effort to protect the environment and the habitats of endangered wildlife.

Maathai Wangari, environmentalist and founder of the Green Belt Movement in Kenya.

## Kenya
### Nanyuki River in Rift Valley Province

**Issue**   The Nanyuki river has become shallow and the water is stagnant and dirty.
Local residents rely on river water for domestic use, livestock and farming.

**Causes**  Large scale removal of forest from the river banks and surrounding hills mainly for fuel.

**Effect**  Evaporation of the river water.

**Action**  **River Management**
• Reforestation is essential.
• Local people need to be encouraged to plant more trees.
• Businesses need to be re-located further from the river to reduce pollution of its waters.
• Irrigation needs to be controlled.

**On-going concerns**
• There is a lack of alternative sources of fuel.
• Climate change has resulted in a loss of snow and ice on the mountain tops.

## Uganda
### Co-operative farming of organic cotton in Northern Uganda

**Issue**   Degradation of soils in Northern Uganda.

**Cause**   Mis-management of land and poor farming practices.

**Action**  • Investment by international organisation in organic cotton farming.
• Introduction of crop rotation to include food crops.
• Use of organic pesticides.

**Result**  • High yield of organic cotton crops.
• Increase in production of food crops such as millet, maize and beans.
• Re-vitalisation of local economy.
• Northern Uganda is now a hub for cotton growing.
• About 24 000 farmers are now growing organic cotton in Lira District.

## Tanzania
### Receding icecap of Mount Kilimanjaro

These two images illustrate the changes over time in snow cover at the summit of Mount Kilimanjaro. Ice on the summit has shrunk gradually over the past century. Most scientists forecast that the glaciers of Mount Kilimanjaro will be gone by the year 2020. This could be due to climate change and climatologists are currently studying weather trends and environmental changes.

The loss of Kilimanjaro's permanent icecap will impact on local populations who depend on access to melt water from the ice fields for fresh water during dry seasons and monsoon failures.

Ice fields on top of Kilimanjaro 1993

Ice fields on top of Kilimanjaro 2000

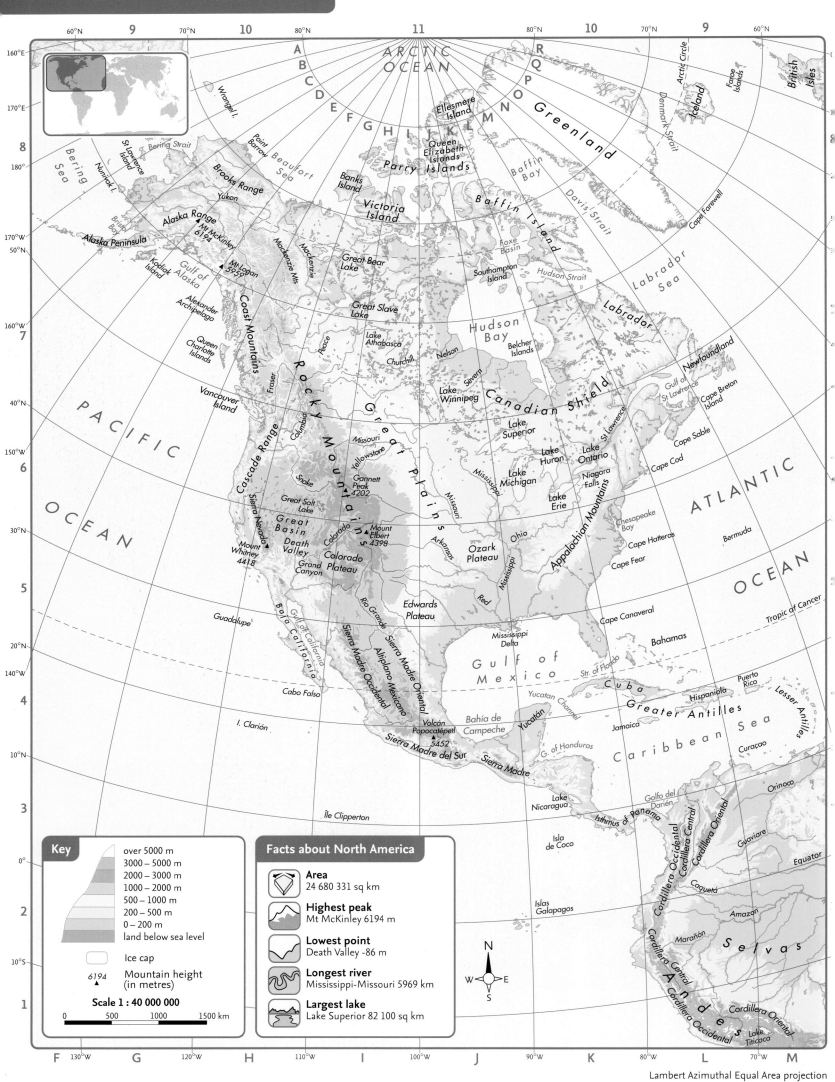

Key

over 5000 m
3000 – 5000 m
2000 – 3000 m
1000 – 2000 m
500 – 1000 m
200 – 500 m
0 – 200 m
land below sea level

Ice cap

6194 ▲ Mountain height
(in metres)

**Scale 1 : 40 000 000**

0          500          1000          1500 km

**Facts about North America**

**Area**
24 680 331 sq km

**Highest peak**
Mt McKinley 6194 m

**Lowest point**
Death Valley -86 m

**Longest river**
Mississippi-Missouri 5969 km

**Largest lake**
Lake Superior 82 100 sq km

Lambert Azimuthal Equal Area projection

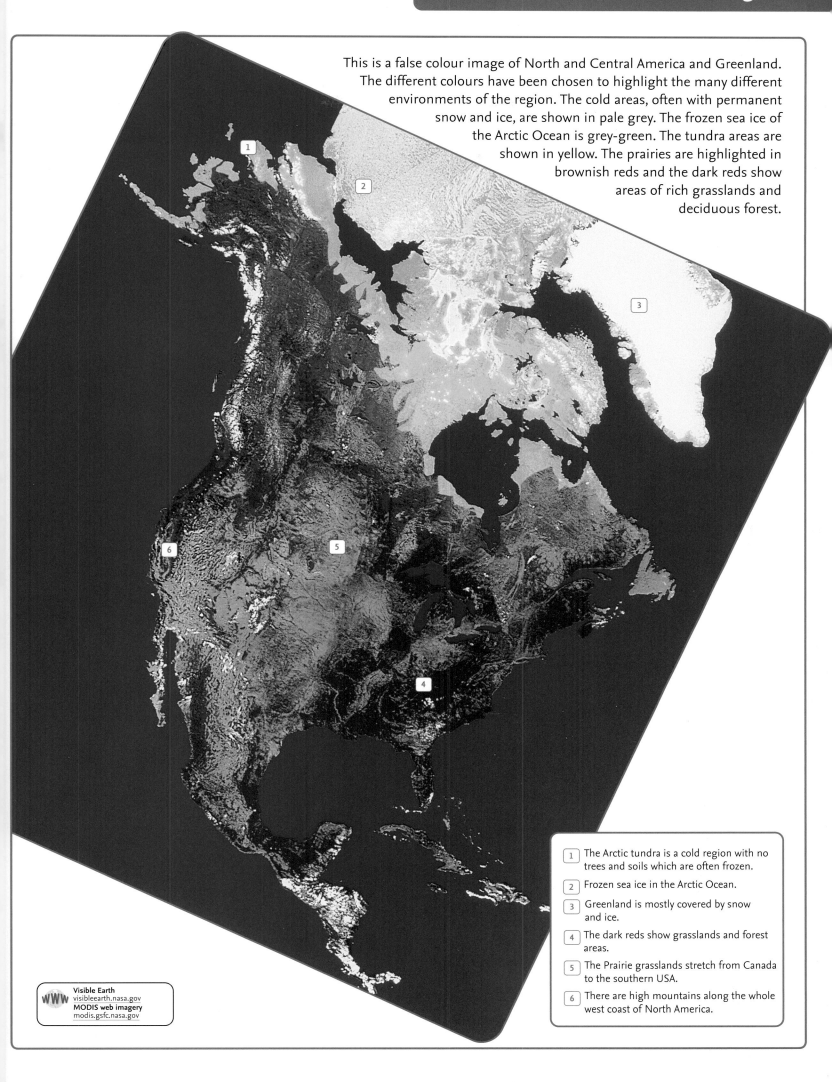

This is a false colour image of North and Central America and Greenland. The different colours have been chosen to highlight the many different environments of the region. The cold areas, often with permanent snow and ice, are shown in pale grey. The frozen sea ice of the Arctic Ocean is grey-green. The tundra areas are shown in yellow. The prairies are highlighted in brownish reds and the dark reds show areas of rich grasslands and deciduous forest.

1. The Arctic tundra is a cold region with no trees and soils which are often frozen.

2. Frozen sea ice in the Arctic Ocean.

3. Greenland is mostly covered by snow and ice.

4. The dark reds show grasslands and forest areas.

5. The Prairie grasslands stretch from Canada to the southern USA.

6. There are high mountains along the whole west coast of North America.

**Visible Earth**
visibleearth.nasa.gov
**MODIS web imagery**
modis.gsfc.nasa.gov

ICELAND
Reykjavík
Arctic Circle
Denmark Strait
Greenland Sea
GREENLAND (Denmark)
Kong Christian IX Land
C. Farewell
Nuuk (Godthåb)
Davis Strait
Baffin Bay
Baffin Island
Labrador Sea
St John's
Newfoundland
Gulf of St Lawrence
St Pierre and Miquelon (France)
Cape Breton Island
Happy Valley Goose Bay
Schefferville
Sept-Îles
St Lawrence
Halifax
Cape Sable
Portland
Boston
Providence
New York
Cape Cod
Philadelphia
Baltimore
ATLANTIC

ARCTIC OCEAN
Ellesmere Island
Queen Elizabeth Islands
Devon Island
Parry Islands
Prince of Wales Island
Melville Island
Prince Patrick Island
Banks Island
Victoria Island
Cambridge Bay
Hudson Strait
Foxe Basin
Melville Peninsula
Southampton Island
Belcher Islands
James Bay
Hudson Bay
Canadian Shield
Severn
Churchill
Nelson
Québec
Ottawa
Montréal
Lake Ontario
Albany
Toronto
Lake Erie
Buffalo
Sault Sainte Marie
Lake Huron
Cleveland
Pittsburgh
Lake Superior
Thunder Bay
Lake Michigan
Detroit
Chicago
Columbus
Cincinnati
Indianapolis
Lake Winnipeg
Winnipeg
Duluth
Green Bay
Milwaukee
Minneapolis-St Paul
Sioux Falls
Des Moines
St Joseph
Kansas City
Omaha
Missouri
CANADA

CONUS
Beaufort Sea
Mackenzie
Mackenzie Mountains
Great Bear Lake
Yellowknife
Hay River
Great Slave Lake
Lake Athabasca
Fort McMurray
Reindeer Lake
Churchill
Peace
Lake Manitoba
Saskatoon
Regina
Great Plains
Edmonton
Calgary
Lethbridge
UNITED STATES OF
Dawson Creek
Grande Prairie
Mt Robson 3954
Rocky Mountains
Spokane
Yellowstone
Cheyenne
Denver 4398
Salt Lake City
Great Salt Lake
Boise
Snake
Gannett Peak 4202
Wheeler Peak 3982
Las

RUSSIAN
Wrangel Island
Chukchi Sea
Point Hope
Bering Strait
Anadyr
Chukotskiy Poluostrov
Anadyrskiy Zaliv
St Lawrence Island
FEDERATION
Bering Sea
Brooks Range
U.S.A.
Fairbanks
Yukon
Alaska Range (Alaska Range)
Mount McKinley 6194
Anchorage
Seward
Kodiak Island
Alaska Peninsula
Bristol Bay
Gulf of Alaska
Juneau
Whitehorse
Mount Logan 5959
Coast Mountains
Alexander Archipelago
Prince Rupert
Queen Charlotte Islands
Mount Waddington 4042
Fraser
Churchill Pk 2812
Vancouver
Victoria
Vancouver I.
Seattle
Portland
Eugene
Mount Rainier 4392
Crescent City
Sacramento
San Francisco
San Jose
Mount Shasta 4317
Sierra Nevada
Great Basin
Mount Whitney 4418

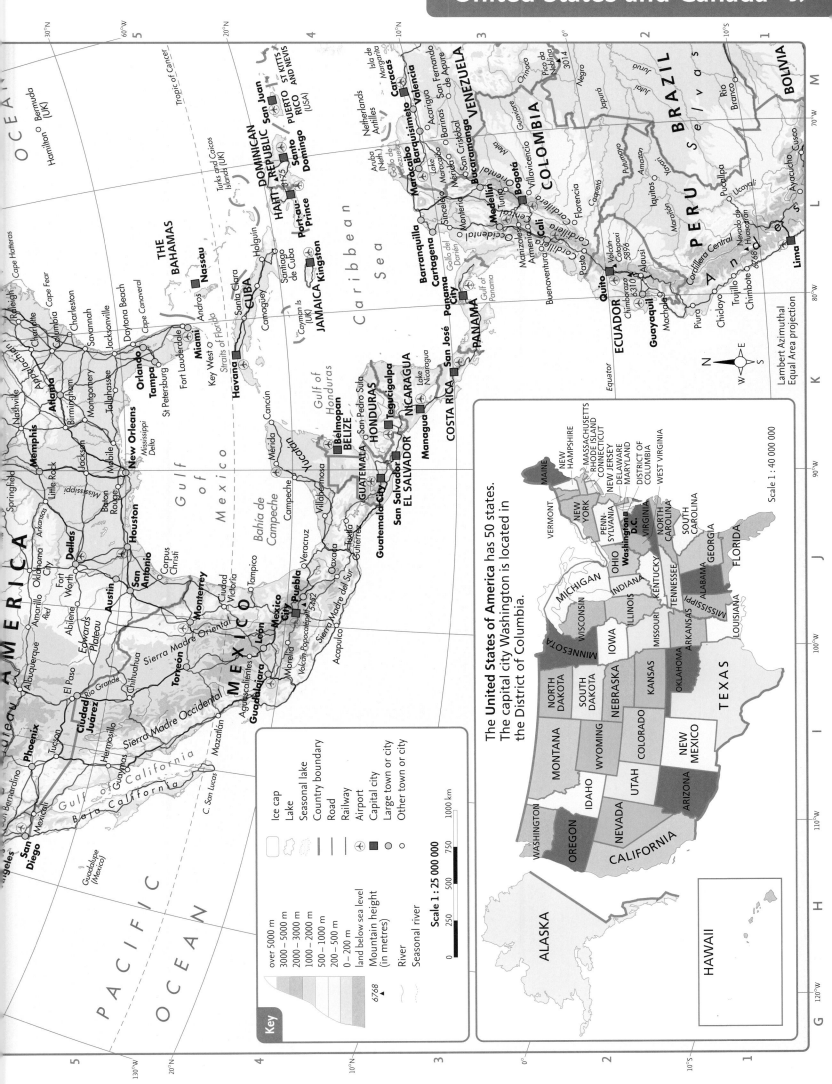

**Key**

| | |
|---|---|
| | Ice cap |
| | Lake |
| | Seasonal lake |
| | Country boundary |
| | Road |
| | Railway |
| ✈ | Airport |
| ■ | Capital city |
| ● | Large town or city |
| ○ | Other town or city |

**Mountain height (in metres)**

- over 5000 m
- 3000 – 5000 m
- 2000 – 3000 m
- 1000 – 2000 m
- 500 – 1000 m
- 200 – 500 m
- 0 – 200 m
- land below sea level

▲ 6768  Mountain height (in metres)

River

Seasonal river

**Scale 1 : 25 000 000**

0  250  500  750  1000 km

The **United States of America** has 50 states.
The capital city Washington is located in
the District of Columbia.

Scale 1 : 40 000 000

Lambert Azimuthal
Equal Area projection

N
W  E
S

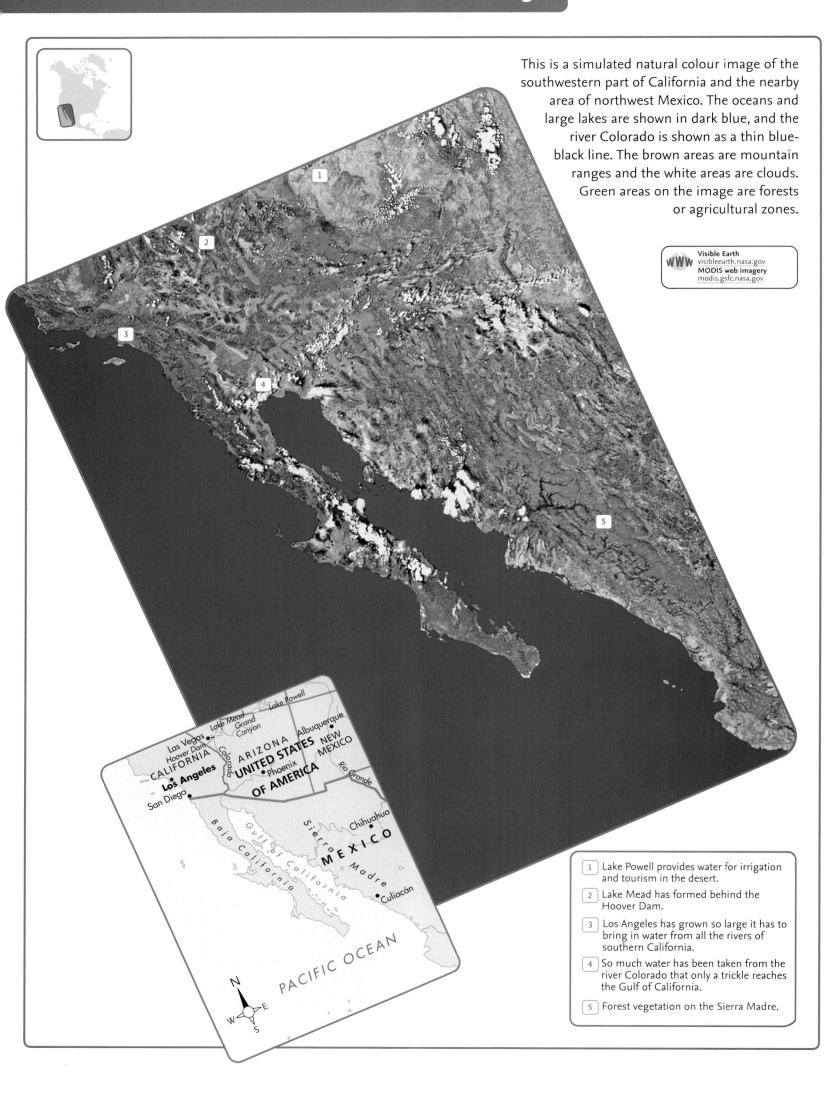

This is a simulated natural colour image of the southwestern part of California and the nearby area of northwest Mexico. The oceans and large lakes are shown in dark blue, and the river Colorado is shown as a thin blue-black line. The brown areas are mountain ranges and the white areas are clouds. Green areas on the image are forests or agricultural zones.

**Visible Earth**
visibleearth.nasa.gov
**MODIS web imagery**
modis.gsfc.nasa.gov

1 Lake Powell provides water for irrigation and tourism in the desert.

2 Lake Mead has formed behind the Hoover Dam.

3 Los Angeles has grown so large it has to bring in water from all the rivers of southern California.

4 So much water has been taken from the river Colorado that only a trickle reaches the Gulf of California.

5 Forest vegetation on the Sierra Madre.

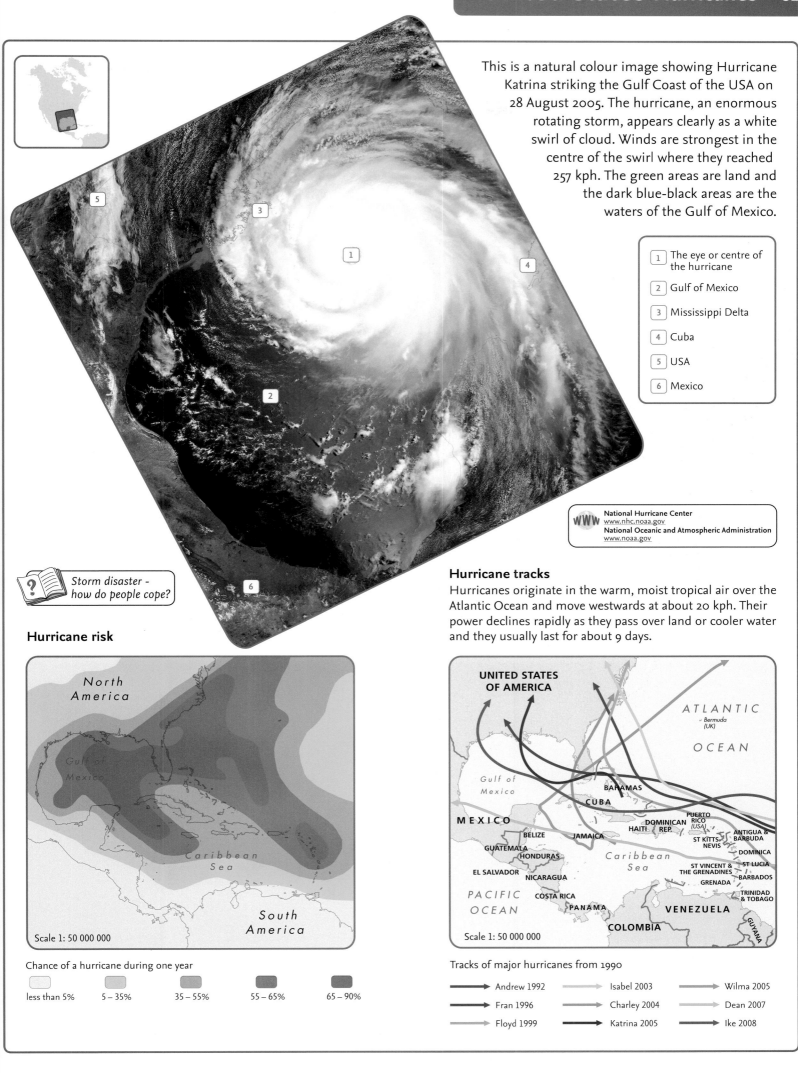

This is a natural colour image showing Hurricane Katrina striking the Gulf Coast of the USA on 28 August 2005. The hurricane, an enormous rotating storm, appears clearly as a white swirl of cloud. Winds are strongest in the centre of the swirl where they reached 257 kph. The green areas are land and the dark blue-black areas are the waters of the Gulf of Mexico.

| | |
|---|---|
| 1 | The eye or centre of the hurricane |
| 2 | Gulf of Mexico |
| 3 | Mississippi Delta |
| 4 | Cuba |
| 5 | USA |
| 6 | Mexico |

**WWW** National Hurricane Center
www.nhc.noaa.gov
National Oceanic and Atmospheric Administration
www.noaa.gov

*Storm disaster - how do people cope?*

## Hurricane tracks

Hurricanes originate in the warm, moist tropical air over the Atlantic Ocean and move westwards at about 20 kph. Their power declines rapidly as they pass over land or cooler water and they usually last for about 9 days.

## Hurricane risk

North America

Gulf of Mexico

Caribbean Sea

South America

Scale 1: 50 000 000

**Chance of a hurricane during one year**

| less than 5% | 5 – 35% | 35 – 55% | 55 – 65% | 65 – 90% |
|---|---|---|---|---|

UNITED STATES OF AMERICA

ATLANTIC OCEAN

Bermuda (UK)

Gulf of Mexico

BAHAMAS

CUBA

MEXICO

PUERTO RICO (USA)

DOMINICAN REP.

HAITI

BELIZE    JAMAICA

GUATEMALA

HONDURAS

ANTIGUA & BARBUDA

ST KITTS-NEVIS

DOMINICA

Caribbean Sea

ST VINCENT & THE GRENADINES

ST LUCIA

EL SALVADOR

NICARAGUA

BARBADOS

GRENADA

PACIFIC OCEAN

COSTA RICA

PANAMA

TRINIDAD & TOBAGO

VENEZUELA

COLOMBIA

GUYANA

Scale 1: 50 000 000

**Tracks of major hurricanes from 1990**

| | | |
|---|---|---|
| Andrew 1992 | Isabel 2003 | Wilma 2005 |
| Fran 1996 | Charley 2004 | Dean 2007 |
| Floyd 1999 | Katrina 2005 | Ike 2008 |

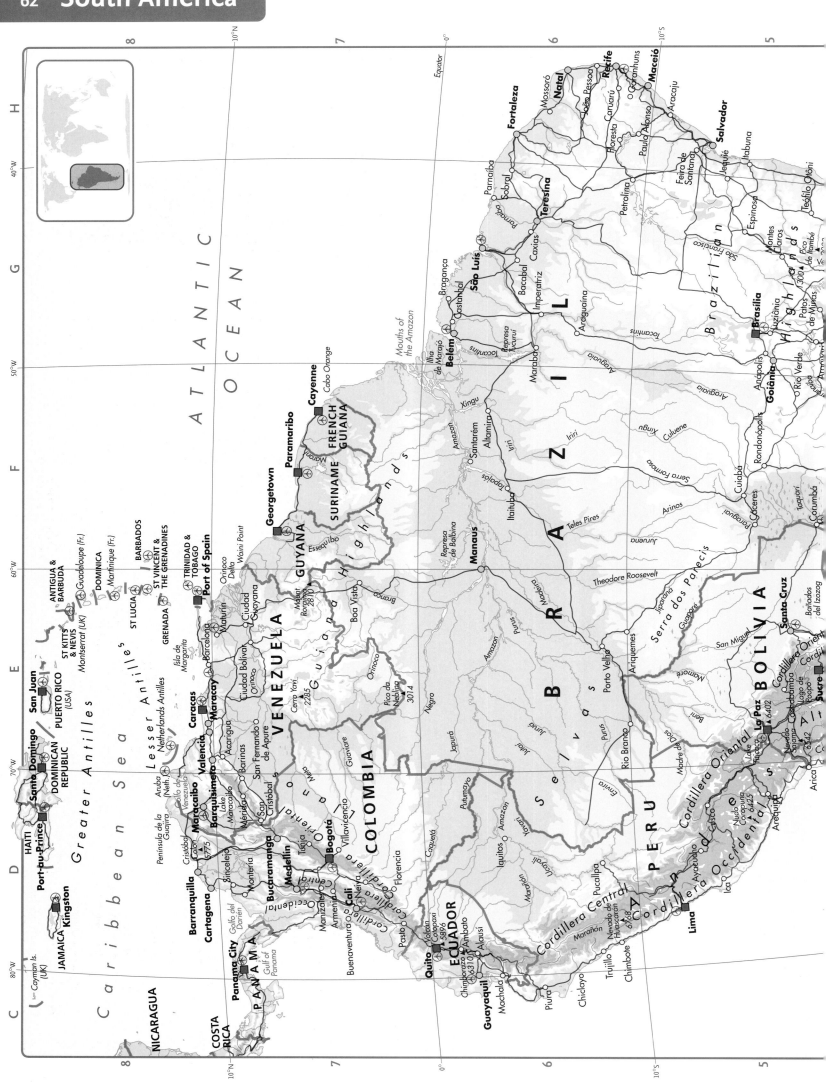

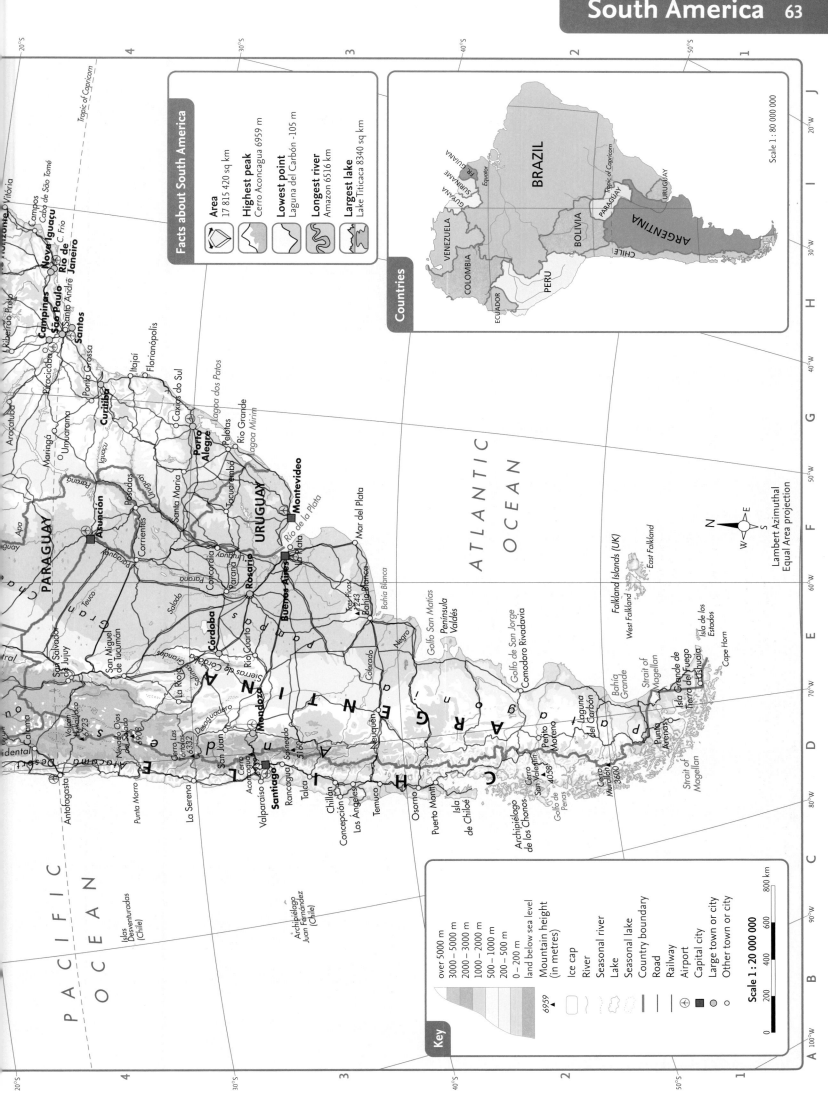

## Facts about South America

**Area**
17 815 420 sq km

**Highest peak**
Cerro Aconcagua 6959 m

**Lowest point**
Laguna del Carbón -105 m

**Longest river**
Amazon 6516 km

**Largest lake**
Lake Titicaca 8340 sq km

## Countries

Scale 1 : 80 000 000

## Key

over 5000 m
3000 – 5000 m
2000 – 3000 m
1000 – 2000 m
500 – 1000 m
200 – 500 m
0 – 200 m
land below sea level

6959 ▲ Mountain height (in metres)

Ice cap
River
Seasonal river
Lake
Seasonal lake
Country boundary
Road
Railway
Airport
Capital city
Large town or city
Other town or city

**Scale 1 : 20 000 000**

0   200   400   600   800 km

N
W   E
S

Lambert Azimuthal
Equal Area projection

PACIFIC OCEAN

ATLANTIC OCEAN

BRAZIL
VENEZUELA
COLOMBIA
ECUADOR
PERU
BOLIVIA
PARAGUAY
CHILE
ARGENTINA
URUGUAY
GUYANA
SURINAME
FR. GUIANA

Equator
Tropic of Capricorn

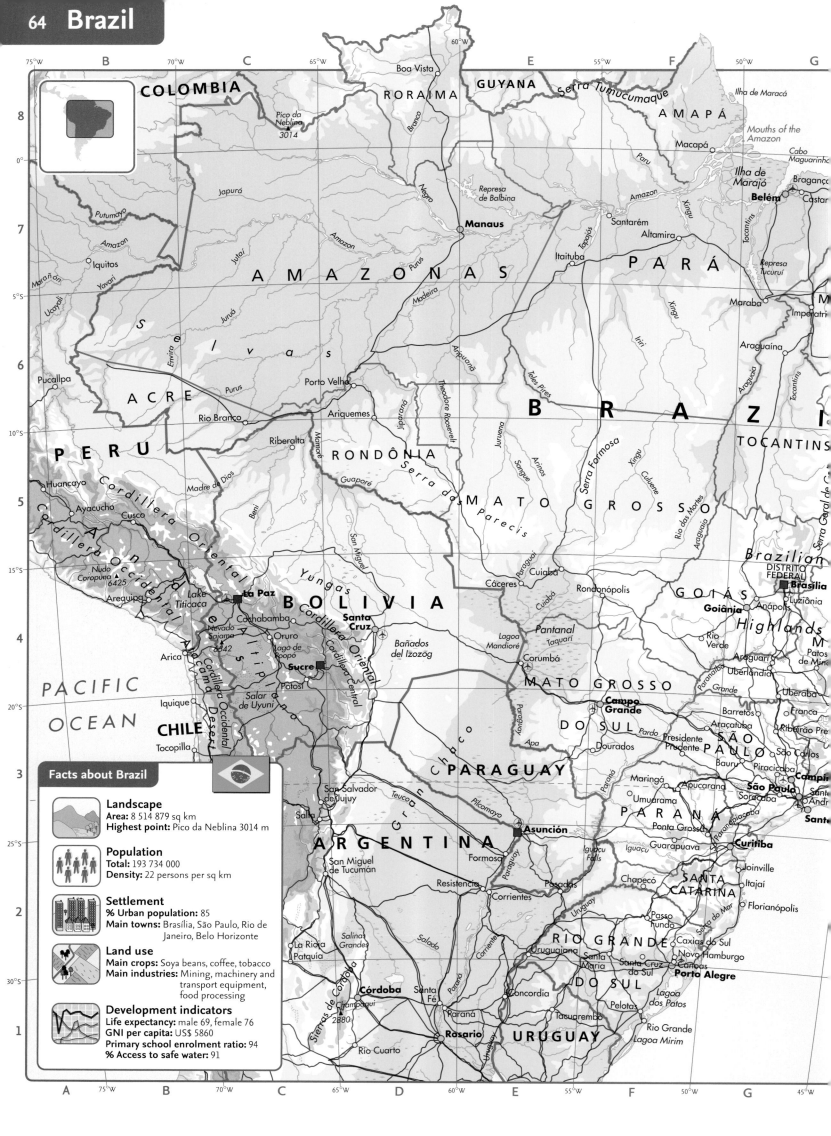

## Facts about Brazil

**Landscape**
Area: 8 514 879 sq km
Highest point: Pico da Neblina 3014 m

**Population**
Total: 193 734 000
Density: 22 persons per sq km

**Settlement**
% Urban population: 85
Main towns: Brasília, São Paulo, Rio de Janeiro, Belo Horizonte

**Land use**
Main crops: Soya beans, coffee, tobacco
Main industries: Mining, machinery and transport equipment, food processing

**Development indicators**
Life expectancy: male 69, female 76
GNI per capita: US$ 5860
Primary school enrolment ratio: 94
% Access to safe water: 91

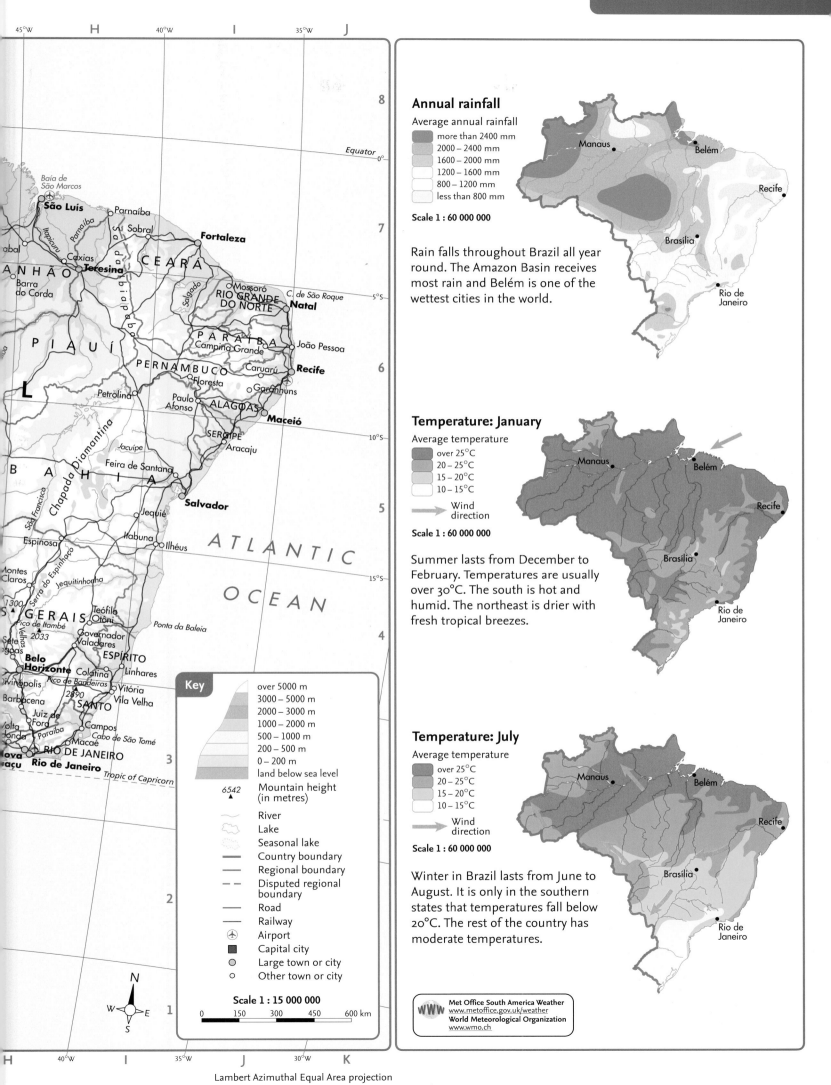

45°W  H  40°W  I  35°W  J

Equator 0°

8

7

5°S

6

10°S

ATLANTIC

15°S

OCEAN

5

4

Tropic of Capricorn

3

2

1

**Key**

over 5000 m
3000 – 5000 m
2000 – 3000 m
1000 – 2000 m
500 – 1000 m
200 – 500 m
0 – 200 m
land below sea level

6542 ▲ Mountain height (in metres)

River
Lake
Seasonal lake
Country boundary
Regional boundary
Disputed regional boundary
Road
Railway
✈ Airport
■ Capital city
◉ Large town or city
○ Other town or city

**Scale 1 : 15 000 000**

0    150    300    450    600 km

N
W E
S

H  40°W  I  35°W  J  30°W  K

Lambert Azimuthal Equal Area projection

## Annual rainfall

Average annual rainfall

more than 2400 mm
2000 – 2400 mm
1600 – 2000 mm
1200 – 1600 mm
800 – 1200 mm
less than 800 mm

Scale 1 : 60 000 000

Rain falls throughout Brazil all year round. The Amazon Basin receives most rain and Belém is one of the wettest cities in the world.

## Temperature: January

Average temperature

over 25°C
20 – 25°C
15 – 20°C
10 – 15°C
→ Wind direction

Scale 1 : 60 000 000

Summer lasts from December to February. Temperatures are usually over 30°C. The south is hot and humid. The northeast is drier with fresh tropical breezes.

## Temperature: July

Average temperature

over 25°C
20 – 25°C
15 – 20°C
10 – 15°C
→ Wind direction

Scale 1 : 60 000 000

Winter in Brazil lasts from June to August. It is only in the southern states that temperatures fall below 20°C. The rest of the country has moderate temperatures.

**www** Met Office South America Weather
www.metoffice.gov.uk/weather
**World Meteorological Organization**
www.wmo.ch

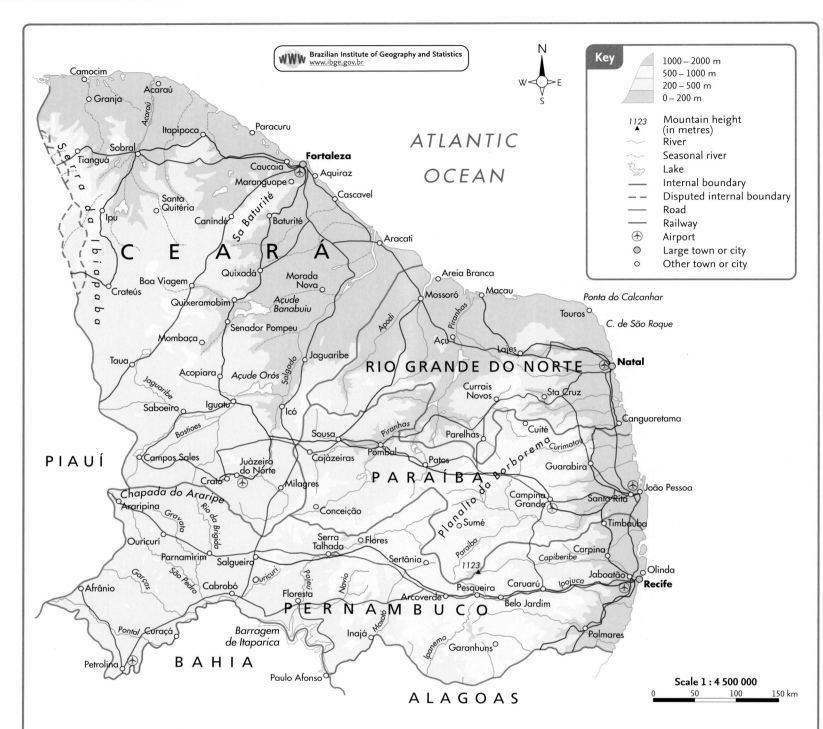

Brazilian Institute of Geography and Statistics
www.ibge.gov.br

**Key**

| | 1000 – 2000 m |
| | 500 – 1000 m |
| | 200 – 500 m |
| | 0 – 200 m |

1123 ▲ Mountain height (in metres)
⌇ River
⌇ Seasonal river
🗺 Lake
── Internal boundary
- - - Disputed internal boundary
── Road
── Railway
✈ Airport
● Large town or city
○ Other town or city

**Scale 1 : 4 500 000**

0    50    100    150 km

*Lambert Azimuthal Equal Area projection*

## Population

Since the 1960s the growth of population has been constant. Most of the population live on or near the coast.

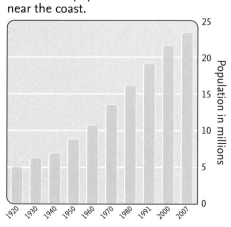

Population in millions

1920 1930 1940 1950 1960 1970 1980 1991 2000 2007

## Employment

Northeast Brazil provides few employment opportunities in the manufacturing sector. Nearly 80% of the workforce are employed in the service industry.

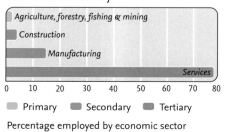

Agriculture, forestry, fishing & mining
Construction
Manufacturing
Services

0  10  20  30  40  50  60  70  80

■ Primary   ■ Secondary   ■ Tertiary

Percentage employed by economic sector

**Facts about Northeast Coast**

**Landscape**
Area: 356 375 sq km
Highest point: 1123 m

**Population**
Total: 23 325 807
Density: 65 persons per sq km

**Settlement**
% Urban population: 74
Main towns/cities: Recife, Fortaleza, Natal

**Land use**
Main crops: Haricot beans, maize, sugar cane, cashew nuts
Main industries: Engineering, chemicals, textiles, food processing

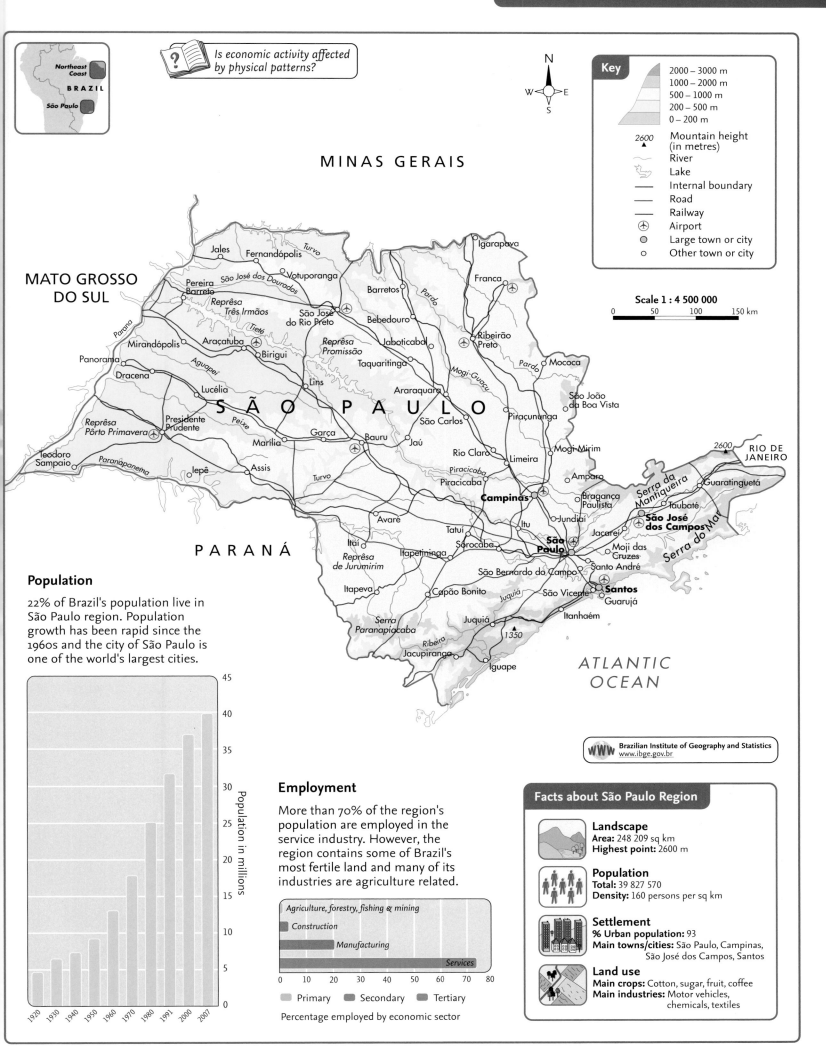

Is economic activity affected by physical patterns?

MINAS GERAIS

MATO GROSSO DO SUL

SÃO PAULO

PARANÁ

RIO DE JANEIRO

ATLANTIC OCEAN

## Key

| | 2000 – 3000 m |
| --- | --- |
| | 1000 – 2000 m |
| | 500 – 1000 m |
| | 200 – 500 m |
| | 0 – 200 m |

▲ 2600 Mountain height (in metres)
River
Lake
Internal boundary
Road
Railway
✈ Airport
⦿ Large town or city
○ Other town or city

Scale 1 : 4 500 000

0    50    100    150 km

**Brazilian Institute of Geography and Statistics**
www.ibge.gov.br

## Population

22% of Brazil's population live in São Paulo region. Population growth has been rapid since the 1960s and the city of São Paulo is one of the world's largest cities.

## Employment

More than 70% of the region's population are employed in the service industry. However, the region contains some of Brazil's most fertile land and many of its industries are agriculture related.

Agriculture, forestry, fishing & mining
Construction
Manufacturing
Services

0   10   20   30   40   50   60   70   80

Primary    Secondary    Tertiary

Percentage employed by economic sector

Population in millions

1920 1930 1940 1950 1960 1970 1980 1991 2000 2007

## Facts about São Paulo Region

**Landscape**
Area: 248 209 sq km
Highest point: 2600 m

**Population**
Total: 39 827 570
Density: 160 persons per sq km

**Settlement**
% Urban population: 93
Main towns/cities: São Paulo, Campinas, São José dos Campos, Santos

**Land use**
Main crops: Cotton, sugar, fruit, coffee
Main industries: Motor vehicles, chemicals, textiles

Lambert Azimuthal Equal Area projection

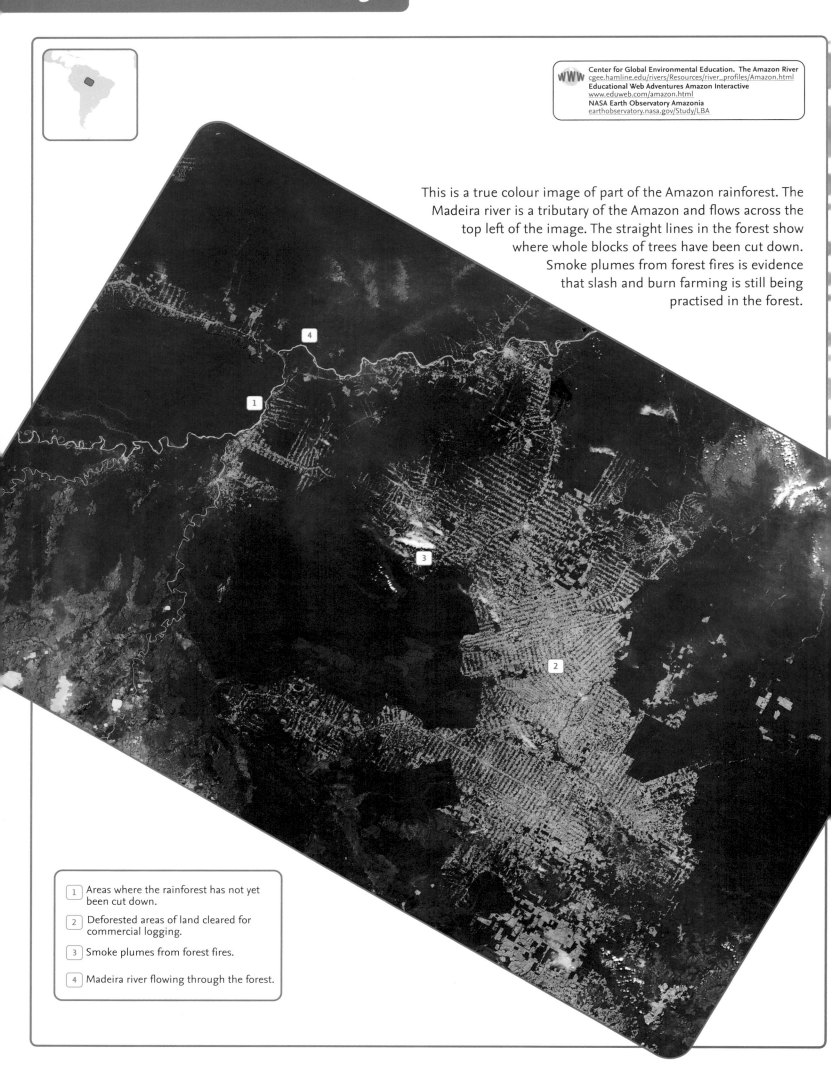

This is a true colour image of part of the Amazon rainforest. The Madeira river is a tributary of the Amazon and flows across the top left of the image. The straight lines in the forest show where whole blocks of trees have been cut down. Smoke plumes from forest fires is evidence that slash and burn farming is still being practised in the forest.

1 Areas where the rainforest has not yet been cut down.

2 Deforested areas of land cleared for commercial logging.

3 Smoke plumes from forest fires.

4 Madeira river flowing through the forest.

## Amazonia : Development

The largest tropical rainforest in the world is in Amazonia in Brazil. Most deforestation has taken place on the edges of the forest in the east, south and southwest. Satellite images like the one opposite allow the Brazilian government to monitor damage to the forest and take steps to prevent unnecessary exploitation of the forest.

☐   Location of satellite image shown on page 68

**HEP developments**
▬   HEP Dam
▬   HEP Dam (planned)

**Communications**
━━━   Railway
-----   Railway (planned)
━━━   Road
-----   Road (planned)

**Land Use**
Cropland and woodland
Grassland and grazing
Grassland and woodland
Tropical forest
Temperate forest
Scrubland or desert
Swamp or marsh
Deforestation
Extent of Amazonia in Brazil

Scale 1 : 30 000 000

*Development or destruction?*

Rainforest clearance takes place to make way for industry.

## Brazil : Resources

Brazil has a wide variety of mineral resources. It produces high grade manganese and iron ore which are its main exports. Industry is concentrated around the main cities where over 85% of the population live.

**Minerals and fuel**
■   Iron ore
■   Tin
●   Manganese
✕   Bauxite
●   Gold
◆   Diamonds
▲   Lead and Zinc
◆   Copper
■   Chromium
◆   Nickel
Coalfield
Oilfield and oilsand
Gasfield
Oil pipeline
Gas pipeline

**Industry**
Iron / Steel
Oil refineries
Shipbuilding
Aircraft
Mechanical engineering
Electronics
Publishing / Paper
Chemicals
Textiles / Clothing
Food processing
●   Major industrial centre

Scale 1 : 30 000 000

**WWW** Brazilian Institute of Geography and Statistics
www.ibge.gov.br

**Key**

| | |
|---|---|
| over 5000 m | |
| 3000 – 5000 m | |
| 2000 – 3000 m | |
| 1000 – 2000 m | |
| 500 – 1000 m | |
| 200 – 500 m | |
| 0 – 200 m | |
| land below sea level | |

5030 ▲ Mountain height (in metres)

~~~ River

~~~ Seasonal river

| | |
|---|---|
| Lake | |
| Seasonal lake | |
| Country boundary | |
| Regional boundary | |
| Road | |
| Railway | |
| ✈ Airport | |
| ■ Capital city | |
| ◉ Large town or city | |
| ○ Other town or city | |

Scale 1 : 20 000 000

0    200    400    600    800 km

**Facts about Australia, New Zealand and Southwest Pacific**

**Population**
35 369 030

**Largest City**
Sydney 4 427 000

**Largest Country**
Australia 7 682 395 sq km

**Country with most people**
Australia 21 293 000

N
W    E
S

## Bushfires

In Australia bushfires are a serious hazard in the dry season especially in the southeast and southwest of the continent.

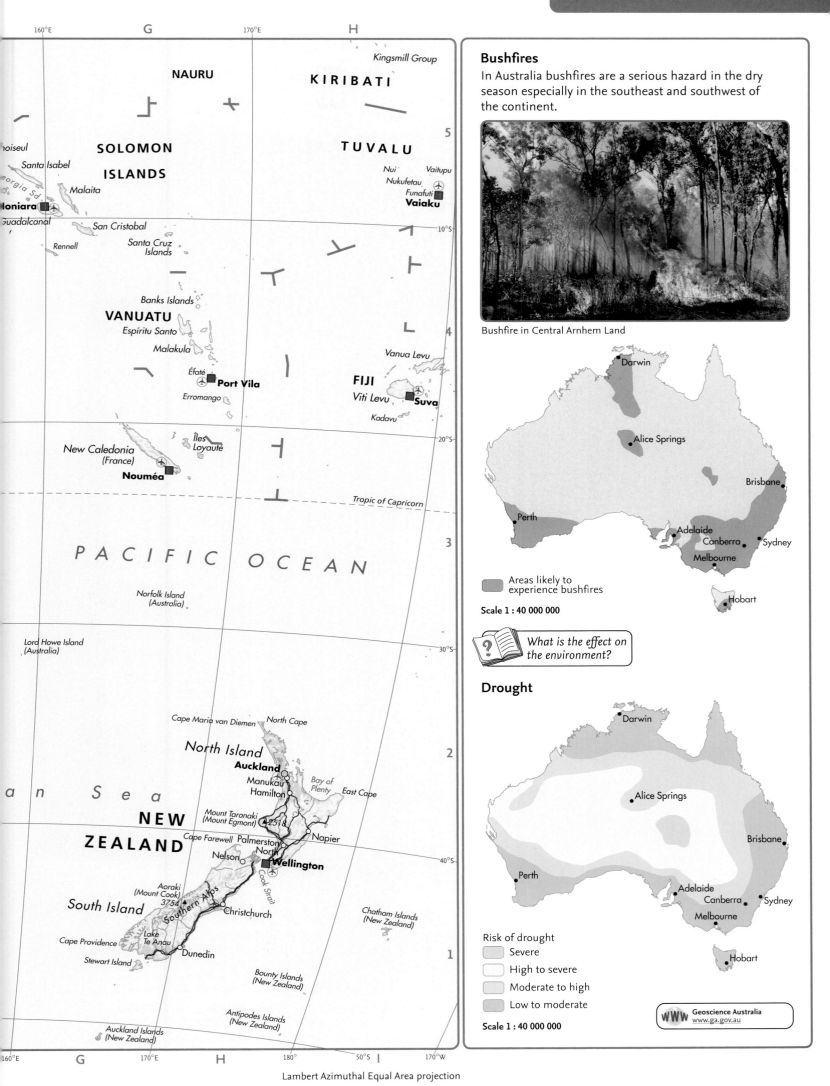

Bushfire in Central Arnhem Land

Areas likely to experience bushfires

Scale 1 : 40 000 000

*What is the effect on the environment?*

## Drought

**Risk of drought**

- Severe
- High to severe
- Moderate to high
- Low to moderate

Scale 1 : 40 000 000

Geoscience Australia
www.ga.gov.au

This is a simulated natural colour image of Australia, New Zealand and the nearby parts of southeast Asia and the southwest Pacific Ocean. The desert of central and western Australia is shown in pink-brown, whilst the greens on the image show those areas with forests and farmland. Areas of grassland are shown in grey-green.

WWW **Visible Earth**
visibleearth.nasa.gov
**MODIS web imagery**
modis.gsfc.nasa.gov

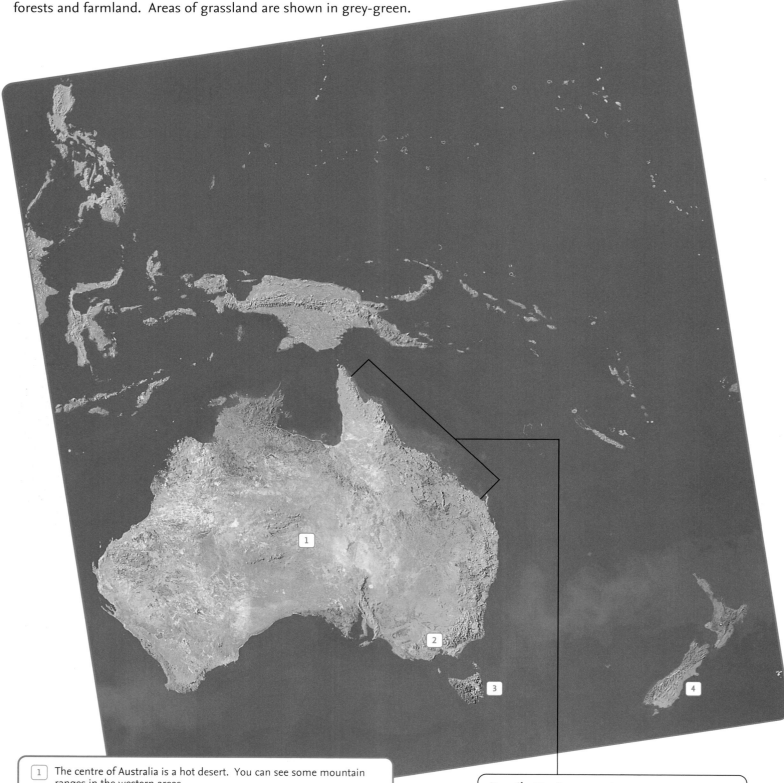

1  The centre of Australia is a hot desert. You can see some mountain ranges in the western areas.

2  Southeast Australia is one of the main farming areas of the country as the green colours show.

3  The island of Tasmania is covered by grassland, forest and farmland.

4  Because New Zealand is further south than Australia it is cooler and wetter. As a result there are more forests.

**Fragile Environment**
The Great Barrier Reef, along the Queensland coast, is the largest barrier reef in the world. The impact of over-fishing, pollution, coral bleaching and sea temperatures rises due to global warming requires action to protect and preserve this unique environment.

## Annual rainfall

Average annual rainfall

- 1000 – 2000 mm
- 500 – 1000 mm
- 250 – 500 mm
- less than 250 mm

**Scale 1 : 60 000 000**

Australia is the driest continent and rainfall is highly variable across the country. The wettest areas are northeast Queensland and southwest Tasmania; the centre of Australia is hot and dry.

## Population

Persons per sq km

- over 50
- 10 – 50
- 1 – 10
- 0 – 1

Cities and towns

- ● 2 500 000 – 5 000 000
- • 1 000 000 – 2 500 000

**Scale 1 : 60 000 000**

Brisbane
Perth
Adelaide
Sydney
Melbourne

Australia has one of the lowest population densities in the world. Distribution is uneven with most people living along the eastern and south eastern coasts. The main urban areas are Adelaide, Brisbane, Melbourne, Perth and Sydney.

## Temperature: January

Average temperature

- over 32°C
- 24 – 32°C
- 16 – 24°C
- 8 – 16°C

→ Wind direction

**Scale 1 : 60 000 000**

Summer lasts from December to February. In January average temperatures exceed 30°C. The hottest areas are northwest Western Australia and from southwest Queensland across south Australia into southeast Western Australia.

**www** World Meteorological Organization
www.wmo.ch
**Met Office Australia Weather**
www.metoffice.gov.uk/weather
**Australian Bureau of Statistics**
www.abs.gov.au

### Where are the people?

## Sydney

Space Imaging

Sydney is Australia's largest city with a population of 4 427 000.

## Temperature: July

Average temperature

- over 24°C
- 16 – 24°C
- 8 – 16°C
- 0 – 8°C
- below 0°C

→ Wind direction

**Scale 1 : 60 000 000**

Winter lasts from June to August. The lowest average temperature is between 7°C in the northwest and 5°C in the southeast. Snow is confined to the mountainous regions of the southeast.

## Facts about Australia

**Landscape**
Area: 7 692 024 sq km
Highest point: Mount Kosciuszko 2229 m

**Population**
Total: 21 293 000
Density: 3 persons per sq km

**Settlement**
% Urban population: 89
Main towns/cities: Sydney, Melbourne, Adelaide, Brisbane, Perth

**Land use**
Main crops: Wheat, sugar, rice, barley
Main industries: Food products, chemicals, transport equipment

**Development indicators**
Life expectancy: male 79, female 84
GNI per capita: US$ 35 760
Primary school enrolment ratio: 96
% Access to safe water: 100

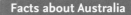

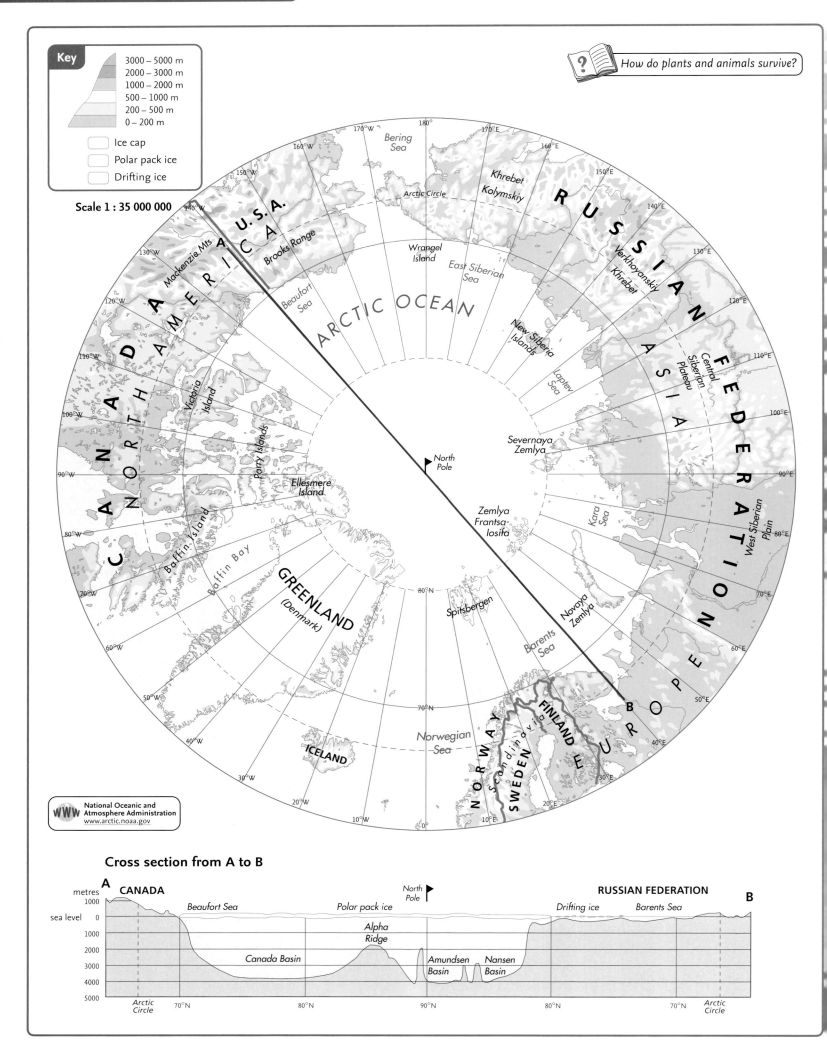

**Key**

| | |
|---|---|
| | 3000 – 5000 m |
| | 2000 – 3000 m |
| | 1000 – 2000 m |
| | 500 – 1000 m |
| | 200 – 500 m |
| | 0 – 200 m |
| | Ice cap |
| | Polar pack ice |
| | Drifting ice |

Scale 1 : 35 000 000

*How do plants and animals survive?*

National Oceanic and
Atmosphere Administration
www.arctic.noaa.gov

Bering
Sea

Khrebet
Kolymskiy

Arctic Circle

RUSSIAN FEDERATION

Wrangel
Island

Verkhoyanskiy
Khrebet

East Siberian
Sea

ARCTIC OCEAN

New Siberia
Islands

Central
Siberian
Plateau

ASIA

Laptev
Sea

Mackenzie Mts

Brooks Range

A M E R I C A

U.S.A.

Beaufort
Sea

North
Pole

Severnaya
Zemlya

West Siberian
Plain

CANADA

N O R T H

Victoria
Island

Parry Islands

Ellesmere
Island

Zemlya
Frantsa-
Iosifa

Kara
Sea

Baffin Island

Baffin Bay

GREENLAND
(Denmark)

80°N

Spitsbergen

Novaya
Zemlya

Barents
Sea

EUROPE

RUSSIAN FEDERATION

70°N

NORWAY

Scandinavia

FINLAND

SWEDEN

Norwegian
Sea

ICELAND

B

**Cross section from A to B**

CANADA

North
Pole

RUSSIAN FEDERATION

| metres | A | | | | | | B |
|---|---|---|---|---|---|---|---|
| 1000 | | Beaufort Sea | | Polar pack ice | | Drifting ice | Barents Sea |
| sea level 0 | | | | | | | |
| 1000 | | | | Alpha Ridge | | | |
| 2000 | | Canada Basin | | | | | |
| 3000 | | | | Amundsen Basin | Nansen Basin | | |
| 4000 | | | | | | | |
| 5000 | | | | | | | |

Arctic Circle — 70°N — 80°N — 90°N — 80°N — 70°N — Arctic Circle

Polar Stereographic projection

## Manned bases in the Antarctic Peninsula

1. Frei (Chile)
2. Comandante Ferraz (Brazil)
3. Bellingshausen (Russian Federation)
4. Jubany (Argentina)
5. Arctowski (Poland)
6. O'Higgins (Chile)
7. Chang Cheng (Great Wall) (China)
8. Artigas (Uruguay)
9. Escudero (Chile)
10. San Martin (Argentina)

Why is Antarctica a fragile environment?

**Key**

- Ice shelf
- Ice cap
- Polar pack ice
- Drifting ice
- Glacier

Scale 1 : 35 000 000

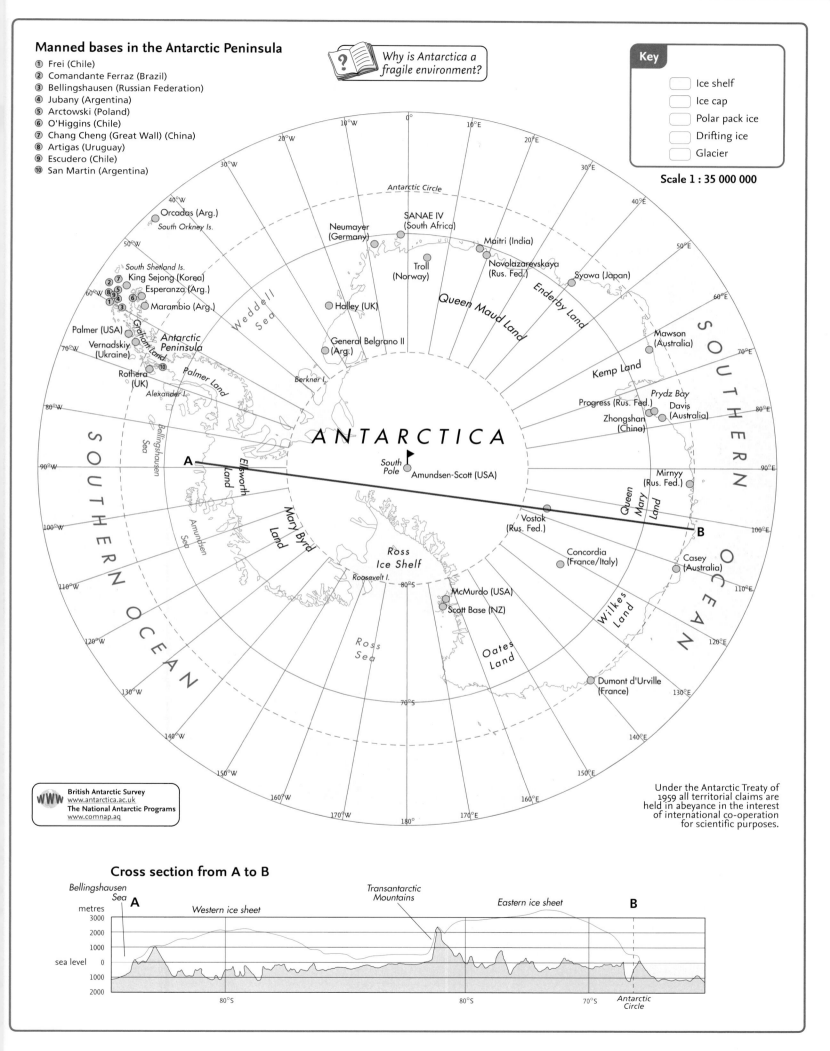

British Antarctic Survey
www.antarctica.ac.uk
The National Antarctic Programs
www.comnap.aq

Under the Antarctic Treaty of 1959 all territorial claims are held in abeyance in the interest of international co-operation for scientific purposes.

### Cross section from A to B

Polar Stereographic projection

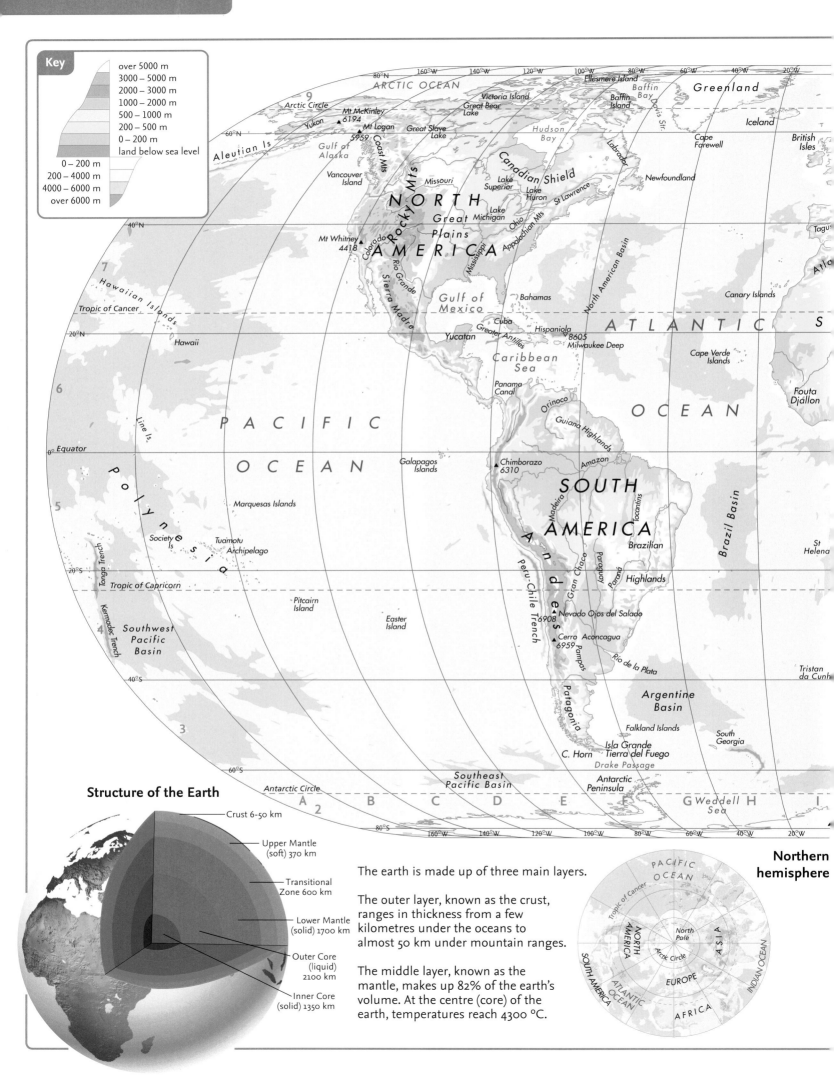

**Key**
- over 5000 m
- 3000 – 5000 m
- 2000 – 3000 m
- 1000 – 2000 m
- 500 – 1000 m
- 200 – 500 m
- 0 – 200 m
- land below sea level

- 0 – 200 m
- 200 – 4000 m
- 4000 – 6000 m
- over 6000 m

ARCTIC OCEAN
Arctic Circle
Greenland
Ellesmere Island
Victoria Island
Great Bear Lake
Baffin Bay
Baffin Island
Iceland
Mt McKinley 6194
Yukon
Mt Logan 5959
Great Slave Lake
Hudson Bay
Davis Str.
British Isles
Aleutian Is
Gulf of Alaska
Coast Mts
Labrador
Cape Farewell
Vancouver Island
Missouri
Canadian Shield
Lake Superior
Lake Michigan
Lake Huron
St Lawrence
Newfoundland
NORTH AMERICA
Rocky Mts
Great Plains
Ohio
Appalachian Mts
North American Basin
Mt Whitney 4418
Colorado
Rio Grande
Mississippi
ATLANTIC
Hawaiian Islands
Tropic of Cancer
Sierra Madre
Gulf of Mexico
Bahamas
Canary Islands
Hawaii
Yucatan
Cuba
Greater Antilles
Hispaniola
8605 Milwaukee Deep
Cape Verde Islands
Tagu
Atla
Caribbean Sea
OCEAN
S
Line Is
PACIFIC
Panama Canal
Orinoco
Guiana Highlands
Fouta Djallon
Equator
OCEAN
Galapagos Islands
Chimborazo 6310
Amazon
SOUTH AMERICA
Marquesas Islands
Polynesia
Madeira
Brazilian
Brazil Basin
Society Is
Tuamotu Archipelago
Andes
Tocantins
St Helena
Peru-Chile Trench
Gran Chaco
Paraguay
Paraná
Brazilian Highlands
Tonga Trench
Tropic of Capricorn
Pitcairn Island
Easter Island
6908
Nevado Ojos del Salado
Cerro Aconcagua 6959
Pampas
Tristan da Cunh
Kermadec Trench
Southwest Pacific Basin
Rio de la Plata
Patagonia
Argentine Basin
Falkland Islands
South Georgia
Isla Grande Tierra del Fuego
C. Horn
Drake Passage
Antarctic Circle
Antarctic Peninsula
Weddell Sea
Southeast Pacific Basin

### Structure of the Earth

- Crust 6–50 km
- Upper Mantle (soft) 370 km
- Transitional Zone 600 km
- Lower Mantle (solid) 1700 km
- Outer Core (liquid) 2100 km
- Inner Core (solid) 1350 km

The earth is made up of three main layers.

The outer layer, known as the crust, ranges in thickness from a few kilometres under the oceans to almost 50 km under mountain ranges.

The middle layer, known as the mantle, makes up 82% of the earth's volume. At the centre (core) of the earth, temperatures reach 4300 °C.

**Northern hemisphere**

PACIFIC OCEAN
Tropic of Cancer
NORTH AMERICA
ASIA
North Pole
Arctic Circle
SOUTH AMERICA
EUROPE
ATLANTIC OCEAN
INDIAN OCEAN
AFRICA

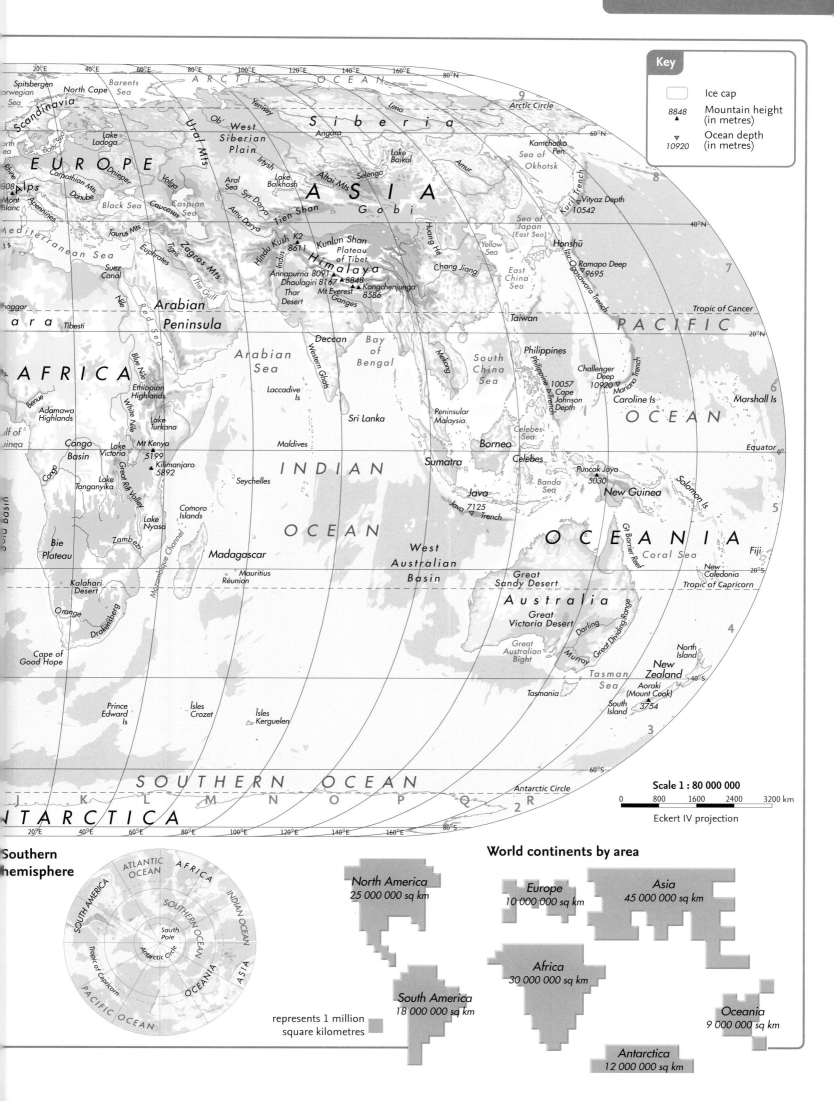

Key
- Ice cap
- ▲ 8848 Mountain height (in metres)
- ▽ 10920 Ocean depth (in metres)

ARCTIC OCEAN

Spitsbergen
Norwegian Sea
North Cape
Barents Sea
Scandinavia
Baltic
Lake Ladoga
Ob'
West Siberian Plain
Irtysh
Yenisey
Angara
S i b e r i a
Lena
Arctic Circle
Kamchatka Pen.
Sea of Okhotsk

EUROPE
Carpathian Mts.
Dnieper
Danube
Volga
Aral Sea
Lake Balkhash
Altai Mts.
Selenga
Lake Baikal
Amur

Alps
Mont Blanc
Apennines
Black Sea
Caucasus
Caspian Sea
A S I A
Gobi
Kuril Trench
Vityaz Depth 10542

Mediterranean Sea
Taurus Mts.
Zagros Mts.
Amu Darya
Syr Darya
Tien Shan
Huang He
Sea of Japan (East Sea)
Honshū
Izu-Ogasawara Trench

Suez Canal
Euphrates
Tigris
The Gulf
Hindu Kush
K2 8611
Kunlun Shan
Plateau of Tibet
Himalaya
Chang Jiang
Yellow Sea
East China Sea
Ramapo Deep ▽ 9695

Nile
Arabian Peninsula
Indus
Annapurna 8091 ▲
Dhaulagiri 8167 ▲ 8848
Thar Desert
Mt Everest 8586
Ganges ▲ Kangchenjunga
Taiwan
PACIFIC

Tibesti
Red Sea
Deccan
Bay of Bengal
Tropic of Cancer

Sahara
AFRICA
Blue Nile
Ethiopian Highlands
Arabian Sea
Western Ghats
South China Sea
Philippines
Challenger Deep 10920 ▽
Mariana Trench
Caroline Is
Marshall Is

Benue
Adamawa Highlands
White Nile
Lake Turkana
Laccadive Is
Sri Lanka
Mekong
Peninsular Malaysia
Philippine Trench
10057 ▽ Cape Johnson Depth
OCEAN

Gulf of Guinea
Congo Basin
Lake Victoria
Mt Kenya ▲ 5199
Maldives
Celebes Sea
Equator

Congo
Lake Tanganyika
Kilimanjaro ▲ 5892
Seychelles
INDIAN
Sumatra
Celebes
Banda Sea
Puncak Jaya ▲ 5030
New Guinea
Solomon Is

Bie Plateau
Lake Nyasa
Zambezi
Java
Java Trench ▽ 7125
OCEANIA

Kalahari Desert
Mozambique Channel
Madagascar
OCEAN
West Australian Basin
Great Barrier Reef
Coral Sea
Fiji

Orange
Comoro Islands
Mauritius
Réunion
New Caledonia
Tropic of Capricorn

Drakensberg
Great Sandy Desert
A u s t r a l i a
Great Dividing Range

Cape of Good Hope
Great Victoria Desert
Darling
North Island

Prince Edward Is
Îles Crozet
Îles Kerguelen
Great Australian Bight
Murray
Tasman Sea
New Zealand
Aoraki (Mount Cook) ▲ 3754

Tasmania
South Island

SOUTHERN OCEAN
Antarctic Circle

ANTARCTICA

Scale 1 : 80 000 000
0  800  1600  2400  3200 km
Eckert IV projection

## Southern hemisphere

ATLANTIC OCEAN
AFRICA
SOUTH AMERICA
SOUTHERN OCEAN
INDIAN OCEAN
South Pole
Antarctic Circle
Tropic of Capricorn
OCEANIA
ASIA
PACIFIC OCEAN

## World continents by area

North America
25 000 000 sq km

Europe
10 000 000 sq km

Asia
45 000 000 sq km

Africa
30 000 000 sq km

South America
18 000 000 sq km

Oceania
9 000 000 sq km

Antarctica
12 000 000 sq km

represents 1 million square kilometres

What do you know about other places?

**Abbreviations of Country Names**

| SOUTH AMERICA | EUROPE | |
|---|---|---|
| **FR.G.** FRENCH GUIANA | **A.** ANDORRA | **MA.** MACEDONIA |
| **GUY.** GUYANA | **ALB.** ALBANIA | **MO.** MOLDOVA |
| **SUR.** SURINAME | **AUS.** AUSTRIA | **NETH.** NETHERLANDS |
| | **BEL.** BELGIUM | **R.F.** RUSSIAN FEDERATION |
| **AFRICA** | **BELA.** BELARUS | **S.** SLOVENIA |
| **B.** BURUNDI | **B.H.** BOSNIA-HERZEGOVINA | **SER.** SERBIA |
| **BE.** BENIN | **CR.** CROATIA | **SL.** SLOVAKIA |
| **BUR.** BURKINA FASO | **CZ.** CZECH REPUBLIC | **SW.** SWITZERLAND |
| **CAM.** CAMEROON | **DEN.** DENMARK | |
| **C.D'I.** CÔTE D'IVOIRE | **EST.** ESTONIA | **ASIA** |
| **EQ. G.** EQUATORIAL | **GER.** GERMANY | **AR.** ARMENIA |
| GUINEA | **H.** HUNGARY | **AZ.** AZERBAIJAN |
| **GH.** GHANA | **K.** KOSOVO | **CYP.** CYPRUS |
| **R.** RWANDA | **LAT.** LATVIA | **GEO.** GEORGIA |
| **T.** TOGO | **LITH.** LITHUANIA | **IS.** ISRAEL |
| | **LUX.** LUXEMBOURG | **JOR.** JORDAN |
| | **M.** MONTENEGRO | **LEB.** LEBANON |
| | | **U.A.E.** UNITED ARAB EMIRATES |

## Time Comparisons

Time varies around the world due to the earth's rotation causing different parts of the world to be in light or darkness at any one time. To account for this, the world is divided into twenty-four Standard Time Zones based on 15° intervals of longitude.

| 1:00am | 2:00am | 3:00am | 4:00am | 5:00am | 6:00am | 7:00am | 8:00am | 9:00am | 10:00am | 11:00am | noon |
|---|---|---|---|---|---|---|---|---|---|---|---|
| Samoa Tonga (next day) | Hawaiian Is Cook Is Tahiti | Anchorage | Vancouver Seattle Los Angeles | Edmonton Phoenix | Winnipeg Chicago Mexico City | New York Miami Lima | Puerto Rico La Paz Asunción | Nuuk Brasília Buenos Aires | South Georgia | Azores Cape Verde | Reykjavík London Freetow |

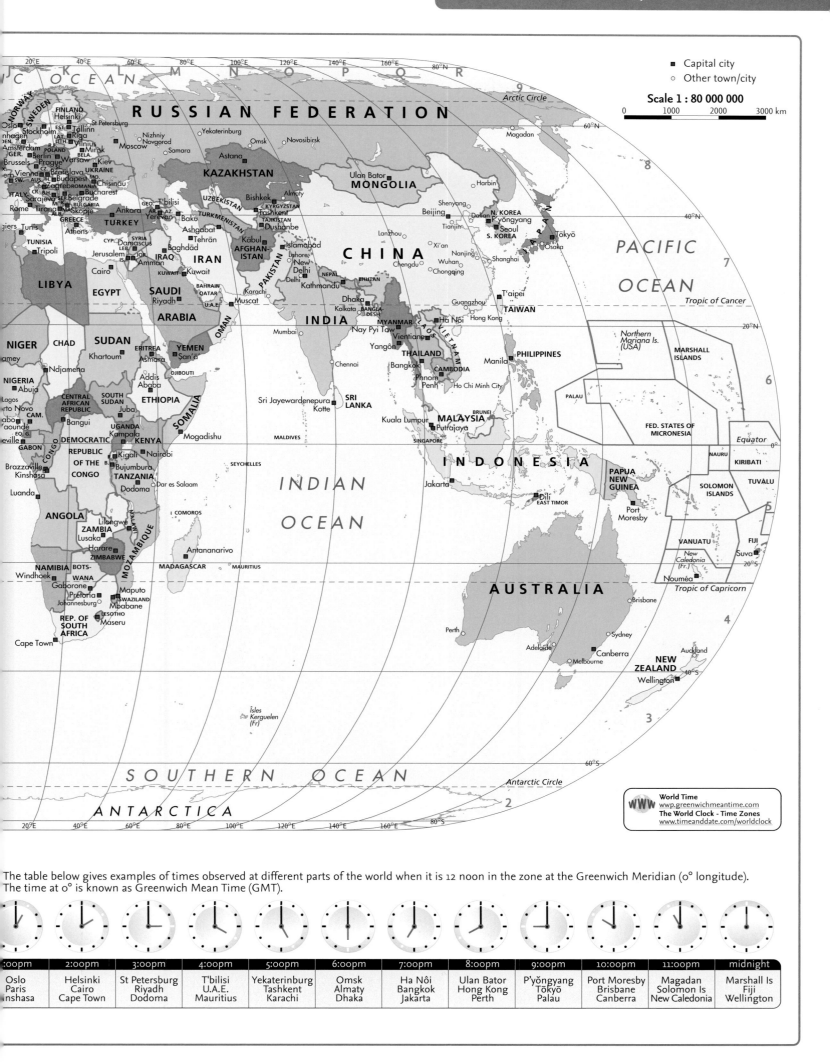

The table below gives examples of times observed at different parts of the world when it is 12 noon in the zone at the Greenwich Meridian (0° longitude). The time at 0° is known as Greenwich Mean Time (GMT).

| 1:00pm | 2:00pm | 3:00pm | 4:00pm | 5:00pm | 6:00pm | 7:00pm | 8:00pm | 9:00pm | 10:00pm | 11:00pm | midnight |
|---|---|---|---|---|---|---|---|---|---|---|---|
| Oslo | Helsinki | St Petersburg | T'bilisi | Yekaterinburg | Omsk | Ha Nôi | Ulan Bator | P'yŏngyang | Port Moresby | Magadan | Marshall Is |
| Paris | Cairo | Riyadh | U.A.E. | Tashkent | Almaty | Bangkok | Hong Kong | Tōkyō | Brisbane | Solomon Is | Fiji |
| Kinshasa | Cape Town | Dodoma | Mauritius | Karachi | Dhaka | Jakarta | Perth | Palau | Canberra | New Caledonia | Wellington |

Eckert IV projection

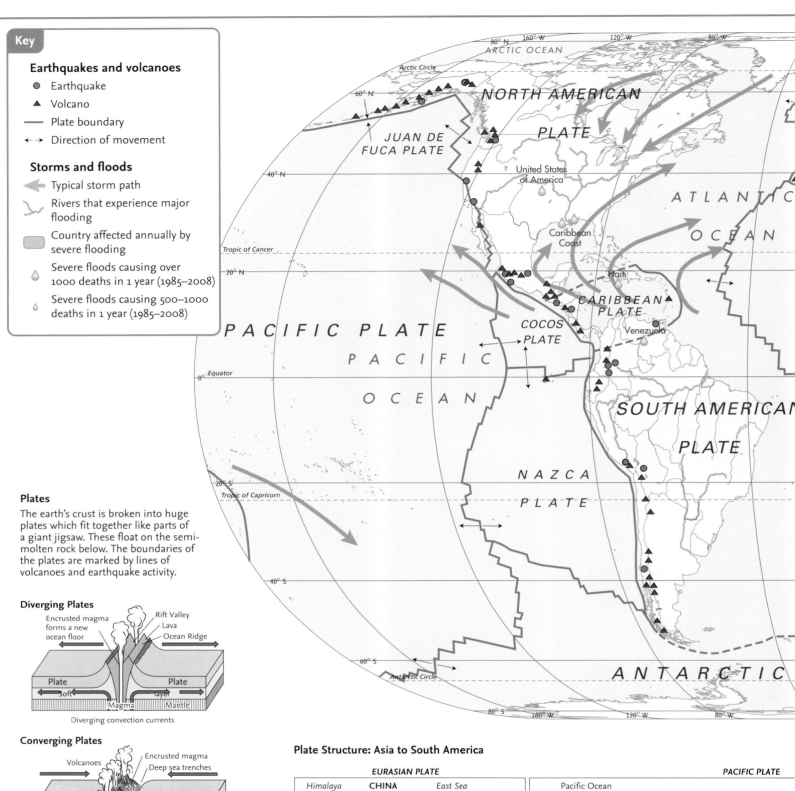

**Key**

**Earthquakes and volcanoes**
- ● Earthquake
- ▲ Volcano
- — Plate boundary
- ←→ Direction of movement

**Storms and floods**
- ← Typical storm path
- ⌇ Rivers that experience major flooding
- ▭ Country affected annually by severe flooding
- ◌ Severe floods causing over 1000 deaths in 1 year (1985–2008)
- ◌ Severe floods causing 500–1000 deaths in 1 year (1985–2008)

**Plates**

The earth's crust is broken into huge plates which fit together like parts of a giant jigsaw. These float on the semi-molten rock below. The boundaries of the plates are marked by lines of volcanoes and earthquake activity.

**Diverging Plates**

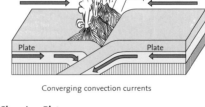

Diverging convection currents

**Converging Plates**

Converging convection currents

**Shearing Plates**

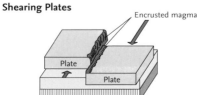

Currents moving past each other

**Plate Structure: Asia to South America**

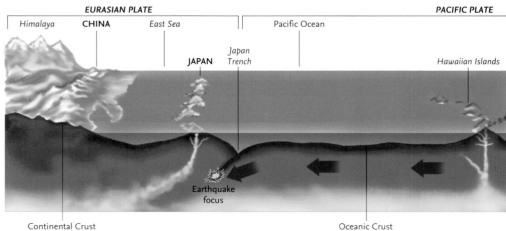

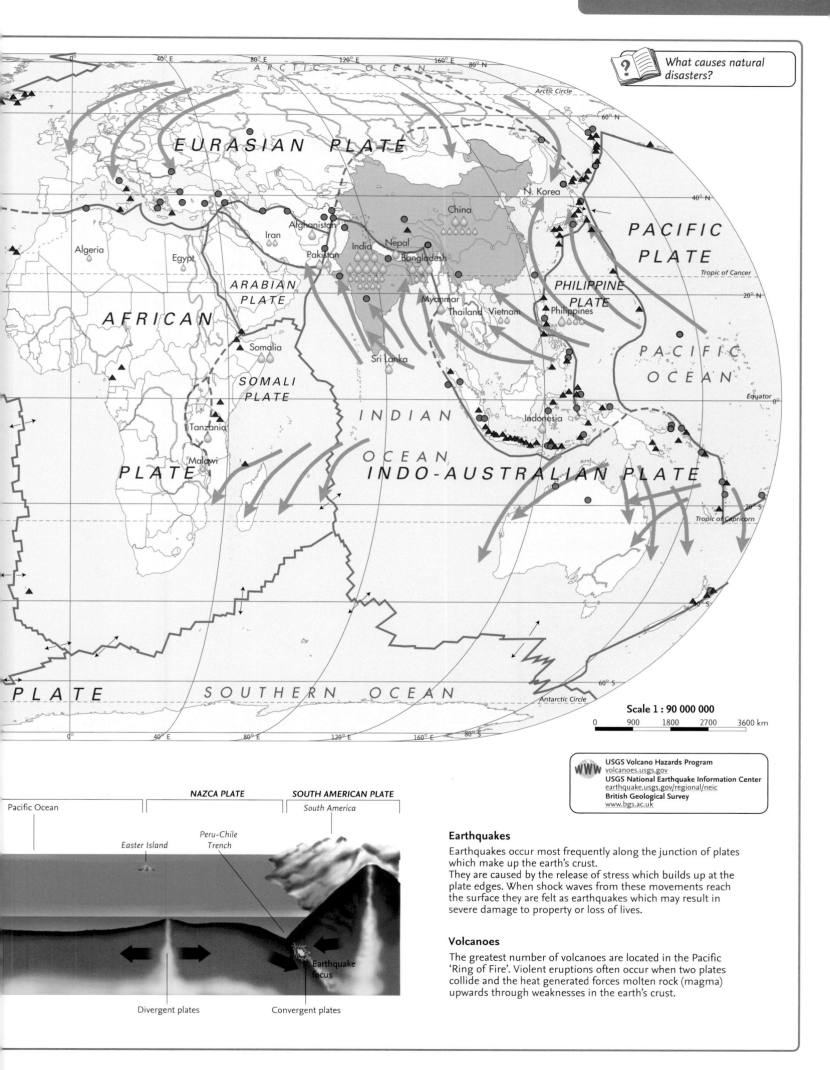

What causes natural disasters?

EURASIAN PLATE

PACIFIC PLATE

PHILIPPINE PLATE

AFRICAN PLATE

ARABIAN PLATE

SOMALI PLATE

INDIAN OCEAN

INDO-AUSTRALIAN PLATE

PACIFIC OCEAN

SOUTHERN OCEAN

Arctic Circle

Tropic of Cancer

Equator

Tropic of Capricorn

Antarctic Circle

Algeria, Egypt, Iran, Afghanistan, Pakistan, India, Nepal, Bangladesh, China, N. Korea, Myanmar, Thailand, Vietnam, Philippines, Sri Lanka, Somalia, Tanzania, Malawi, Indonesia

Scale 1 : 90 000 000

0  900  1800  2700  3600 km

WWW **USGS Volcano Hazards Program**
volcanoes.usgs.gov
**USGS National Earthquake Information Center**
earthquake.usgs.gov/regional/neic
**British Geological Survey**
www.bgs.ac.uk

NAZCA PLATE      SOUTH AMERICAN PLATE

Pacific Ocean      South America

Easter Island

Peru-Chile Trench

Earthquake focus

Divergent plates      Convergent plates

## Earthquakes

Earthquakes occur most frequently along the junction of plates which make up the earth's crust.

They are caused by the release of stress which builds up at the plate edges. When shock waves from these movements reach the surface they are felt as earthquakes which may result in severe damage to property or loss of lives.

## Volcanoes

The greatest number of volcanoes are located in the Pacific 'Ring of Fire'. Violent eruptions often occur when two plates collide and the heat generated forces molten rock (magma) upwards through weaknesses in the earth's crust.

## Climate graphs

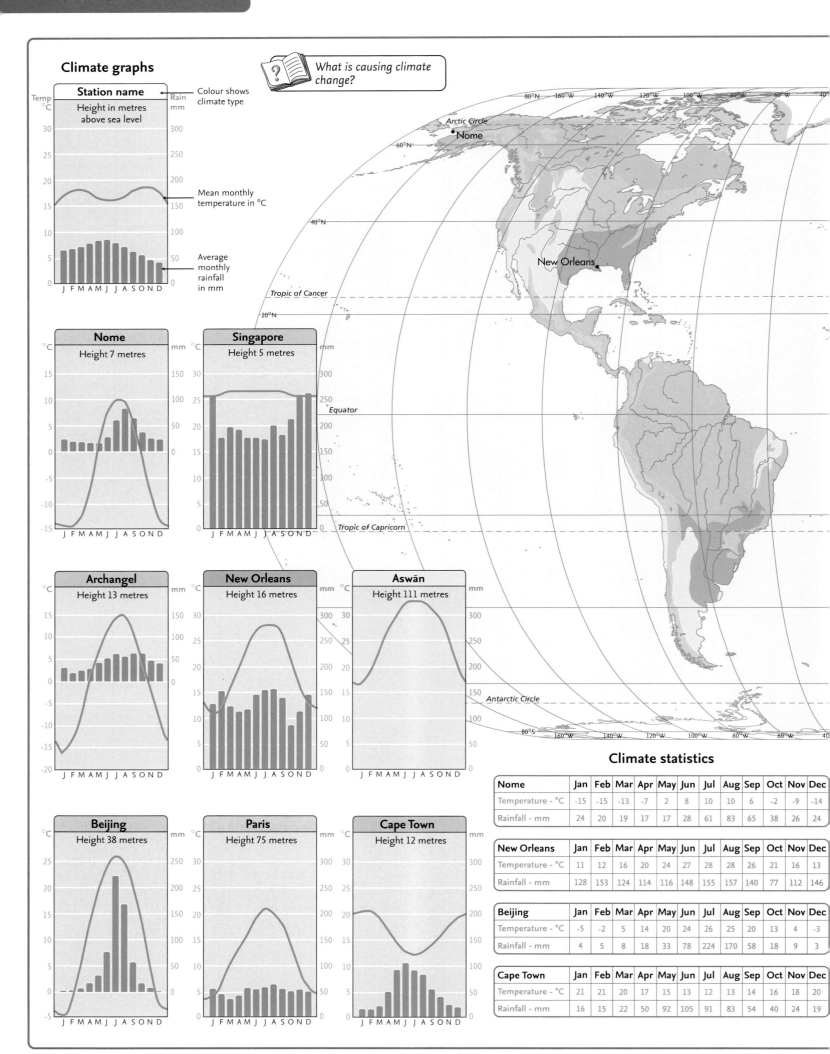

What is causing climate change?

**Station name** — Height in metres above sea level

Colour shows climate type

Mean monthly temperature in °C

Average monthly rainfall in mm

### Climate statistics

| Nome | Jan | Feb | Mar | Apr | May | Jun | Jul | Aug | Sep | Oct | Nov | Dec |
|---|---|---|---|---|---|---|---|---|---|---|---|---|
| Temperature - °C | -15 | -15 | -13 | -7 | 2 | 8 | 10 | 10 | 6 | -2 | -9 | -14 |
| Rainfall - mm | 24 | 20 | 19 | 17 | 17 | 28 | 61 | 83 | 65 | 38 | 26 | 24 |

| New Orleans | Jan | Feb | Mar | Apr | May | Jun | Jul | Aug | Sep | Oct | Nov | Dec |
|---|---|---|---|---|---|---|---|---|---|---|---|---|
| Temperature - °C | 11 | 12 | 16 | 20 | 24 | 27 | 28 | 28 | 26 | 21 | 16 | 13 |
| Rainfall - mm | 128 | 153 | 124 | 114 | 116 | 148 | 155 | 157 | 140 | 77 | 112 | 146 |

| Beijing | Jan | Feb | Mar | Apr | May | Jun | Jul | Aug | Sep | Oct | Nov | Dec |
|---|---|---|---|---|---|---|---|---|---|---|---|---|
| Temperature - °C | -5 | -2 | 5 | 14 | 20 | 24 | 26 | 25 | 20 | 13 | 4 | -3 |
| Rainfall - mm | 4 | 5 | 8 | 18 | 33 | 78 | 224 | 170 | 58 | 18 | 9 | 3 |

| Cape Town | Jan | Feb | Mar | Apr | May | Jun | Jul | Aug | Sep | Oct | Nov | Dec |
|---|---|---|---|---|---|---|---|---|---|---|---|---|
| Temperature - °C | 21 | 21 | 20 | 17 | 15 | 13 | 12 | 13 | 14 | 16 | 18 | 20 |
| Rainfall - mm | 16 | 15 | 22 | 50 | 92 | 105 | 91 | 83 | 54 | 40 | 24 | 19 |

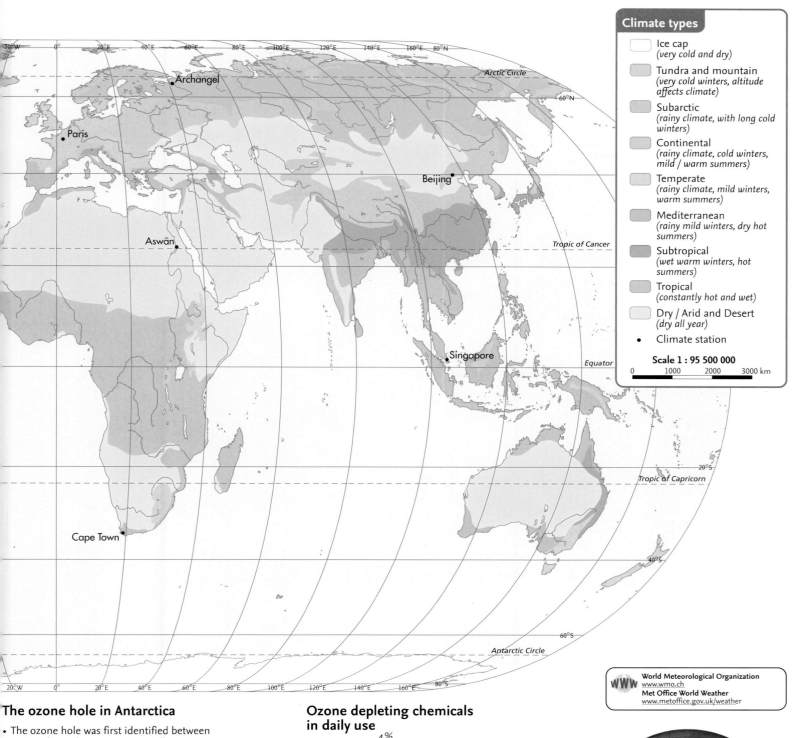

**Climate types**

- Ice cap
  *(very cold and dry)*
- Tundra and mountain
  *(very cold winters, altitude affects climate)*
- Subarctic
  *(rainy climate, with long cold winters)*
- Continental
  *(rainy climate, cold winters, mild / warm summers)*
- Temperate
  *(rainy climate, mild winters, warm summers)*
- Mediterranean
  *(rainy mild winters, dry hot summers)*
- Subtropical
  *(wet warm winters, hot summers)*
- Tropical
  *(constantly hot and wet)*
- Dry / Arid and Desert
  *(dry all year)*
- • Climate station

**Scale 1 : 95 500 000**

0   1000   2000   3000 km

World Meteorological Organization
www.wmo.ch
Met Office World Weather
www.metoffice.gov.uk/weather

## The ozone hole in Antarctica

- The ozone hole was first identified between 1981 and 1983 by scientists at Halley Bay research station.

- The hole begins to develop in August each year – the southern hemisphere's spring – is fully developed by early October and breaks up in early December.

- Compared to the 1970s, by the 1990s, there was a reduction of 60% in ozone level over Antarctica in early October.

- In 2005 the ozone hole covered an area of 27 million square kilometres, more than the combined area of China and the Russian Federation.

- A reduction in the use of CFCs will slow down the thinning of the ozone layer, however, it may take 30 years to recover.

## Ozone depleting chemicals in daily use

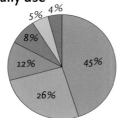

45%
26%
12%
8%
5%
4%

- CFC-12 (aerosols, foams, refrigeration, air conditioning)
- CFC-11 (aerosols, foams, refrigeration)
- CFC-113 (solvents)
- Carbon Tetrachloride (solvents)
- Methyl Chloroform (solvents)
- Halon 1301 (fire extinguishers)

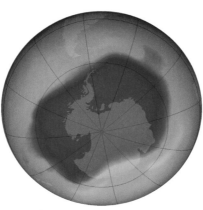

The maximum extent of the ozone hole over Antarctica, 2006

Eckert IV projection

**?** *What is threatened and what are the threats?*

ARCTIC OCEAN

Arctic Circle

51 cu km of ice is lost annually from the Greenland ice cap.

30% of the USA is affected by desertification.

Over 66% of Africa is desert or dryland.

Tropic of Cancer

ATLANTIC

PACIFIC

OCEAN

OCEAN

Equator

The Congo Basin is home to 10 000 types of plants, 400 mammals and 900 varieties of butterfly.

Rainforests which once grew on 14% of the land surface now cover 6%.

Rainforests could disappear completely within 100 years if the current rate of deforestation continues.

Animal habitats are shrinking due to pollution, logging, harmful development and global warming.

Tropic of Capricorn

66% of South America's drylands are desertified.

Antarctic Circle

**Ice cap and ice shelf**
Extremely cold. No vegetation.

**Arctic Tundra**
Very cold climate. Simple vegetation such as mosses, lichens, grasses and flowering herbs.

**Mountain/Alpine**
Very low night-time temperatures. Only a few dwarf trees and small leafed shrubs can grow.

**Mediterranean**
Mild winters and dry summers. Vegetation is mixed shrubs and herbaceous plants.

**Savanna grassland**
Warm or hot climate. Tropical grasslands with scattered thorn bushes or trees.

**Temperate grassland**
Grassland is the main vegetation. Summers are hot and winters cold.

**Desert**
Hot with little rainfall. Very sparse vegetation except cacti and grasses adapted to the harsh conditions.

**Boreal/Taiga forest**
Found between 50° and 70°N. Low temperatures. Vegetation consists of cold tolerant evergreen conifers.

**Coniferous forest**
Dense forests of pine, spruce and larch.

**Temperate forest**
Well defined seasons. Mixture of broadleaf and coniferous trees.

ARCTIC OCEAN

Arctic Circle

60°N

40°N

PACIFIC

Tropic of Cancer

20°N

OCEAN

INDIAN

Equator 0°

OCEAN

20°S

Tropic of Capricorn

40°S

SOUTHERN OCEAN

Antarctic Circle

80°S

**United Nations Environment Programme**
www.unep.org
World Conservation Monitoring Centre
www.unep-wcmc.org
World Resources Institute Earthtrends
earthtrends.wri.org

14 million sq km of Asia is affected by desertification.

90% of Madagascar's forests have been destroyed.

Since the 1700s, 75% of Australia's rainforest has been cleared.

**Scale 1 : 80 000 000**

0    800    1600    2400    3200 km

**Tropical forest**
Dense rainforest found in areas of high rainfall near the equator.

**Dry tropical forest**
Semi deciduous trees with low shrubs and bushes.

**Sub tropical forest**
Rainfall is seasonal. Vegetation is mainly hard leaf evergreen forest.

**Monsoon forest**
Areas which experience Monsoon rain. All trees are deciduous.

## World Ecosystems

million sq km

Evergreen forest · Deciduous forest · Mixed forest · Shrublands · Savannas · Grasslands · Permanent wetlands · Croplands · Urban area · Snow and ice · Sparsely vegetated · Water bodies

Eckert IV projection

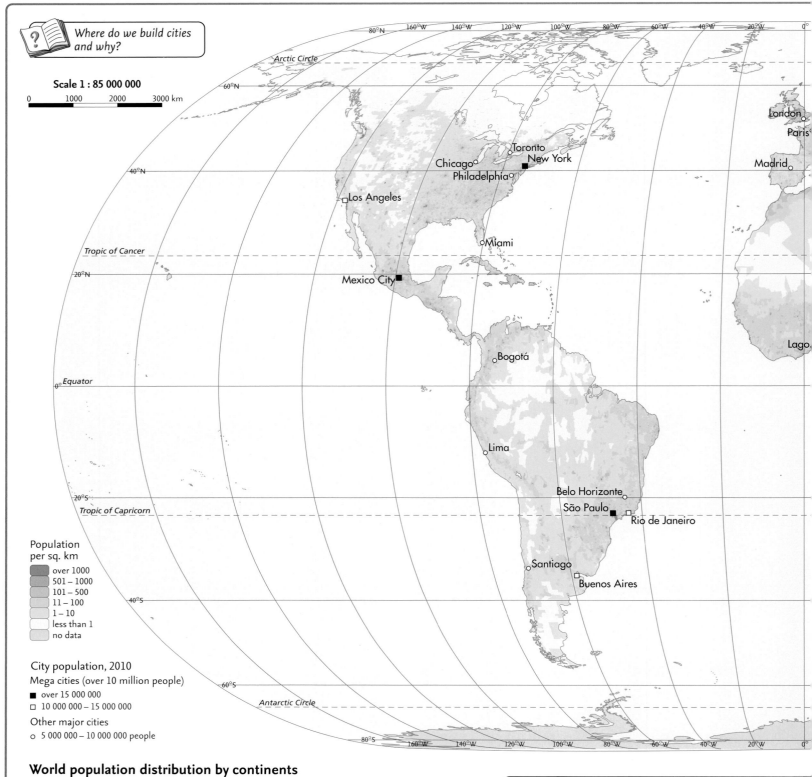

Where do we build cities and why?

**Scale 1 : 85 000 000**

0   1000   2000   3000 km

**Population per sq. km**

- over 1000
- 501 – 1000
- 101 – 500
- 11 – 100
- 1 – 10
- less than 1
- no data

**City population, 2010**

Mega cities (over 10 million people)
- ■ over 15 000 000
- □ 10 000 000 – 15 000 000

Other major cities
- ○ 5 000 000 – 10 000 000 people

## World population distribution by continents

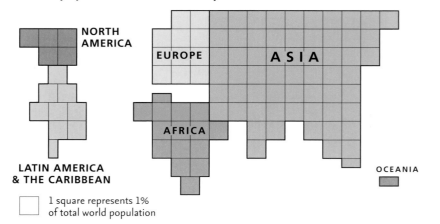

NORTH AMERICA

EUROPE

ASIA

AFRICA

LATIN AMERICA & THE CARIBBEAN

OCEANIA

☐ 1 square represents 1% of total world population

| Facts about world population | |
|---|---|
| World population, 2009 | 6 829 000 000 |
| World population, 2050 | 9 150 000 000 |
| Population over 60 years, 2009 | 10.8% |
| Population over 60 years, 2050 | 21.9% |
| Population under 14 years, 2009 | 27.2% |
| Population under 14 years, 2050 | 19.6% |
| Life expectancy, 2005–2010 | 67 |
| Male life expectancy, 2005–2010 | 65 |
| Female life expectancy, 2005–2010 | 69 |

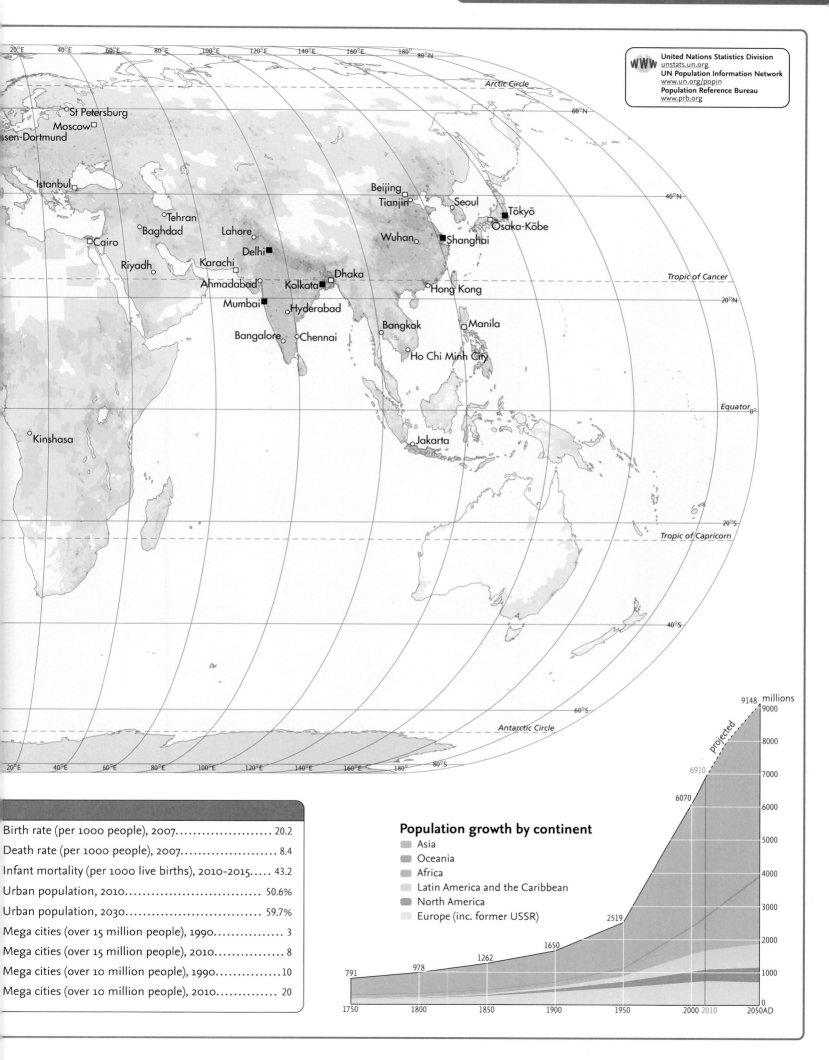

**United Nations Statistics Division**
unstats.un.org
**UN Population Information Network**
www.un.org/popin
**Population Reference Bureau**
www.prb.org

*Arctic Circle*

*Tropic of Cancer*

*Tropic of Capricorn*

*Equator*

*Antarctic Circle*

Cities labelled on map: St Petersburg, Moscow, Essen-Dortmund, Istanbul, Tehran, Baghdad, Cairo, Riyadh, Lahore, Karachi, Delhi, Ahmadabad, Kolkata, Dhaka, Mumbai, Hyderabad, Bangalore, Chennai, Beijing, Tianjin, Wuhan, Shanghai, Seoul, Tōkyō, Osaka-Kōbe, Hong Kong, Bangkok, Manila, Ho Chi Minh City, Jakarta, Kinshasa

| | |
|---|---|
| Birth rate (per 1000 people), 2007 | 20.2 |
| Death rate (per 1000 people), 2007 | 8.4 |
| Infant mortality (per 1000 live births), 2010-2015 | 43.2 |
| Urban population, 2010 | 50.6% |
| Urban population, 2030 | 59.7% |
| Mega cities (over 15 million people), 1990 | 3 |
| Mega cities (over 15 million people), 2010 | 8 |
| Mega cities (over 10 million people), 1990 | 10 |
| Mega cities (over 10 million people), 2010 | 20 |

## Population growth by continent

- Asia
- Oceania
- Africa
- Latin America and the Caribbean
- North America
- Europe (inc. former USSR)

millions

9148
9000
6910
8000
6070
7000
6000
2519
5000
4000
3000
1650
2000
1262
978
791
1000
projected
0

1750   1800   1850   1900   1950   2000 2010   2050AD

Eckert IV projection

## Key

### Desertification

Existing deserts

Areas at risk of desertification

### Deforestation

Existing tropical forests

Forests destroyed since 1940

### Bushfires

Recent major forest fires

### Water pollution

Coastal pollution

River pollution

Major city with air pollution

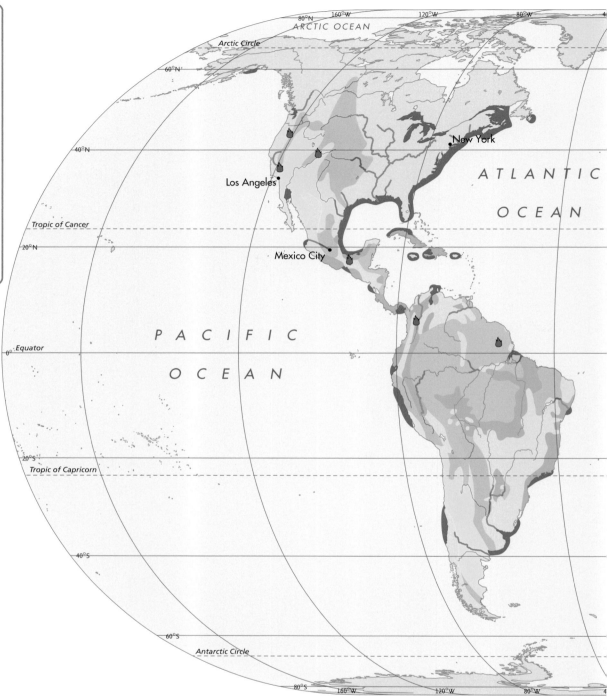

United Nations Environment Programme
www.unep.org
World Conservation Monitoring Centre
www.unep-wcmc.org
World Resources Institute Earthtrends
earthtrends.wri.org
UNESCO World Heritage Sites
whc.unesco.org

### Impacts of deforestation

- Flood water carries away unprotected soil

- Without vegetation to soak up water, heavy rain causes floods

- Without humus from rotting leaves, the soil becomes poorer

- Rivers silt up, causing floods and clogging dams

- Burning trees release $CO_2$ into the atmosphere, adding to 'greenhouse' gases

- Fierce sunshine dries out the earth, making it useless for crops

## Tropical Forest Destruction

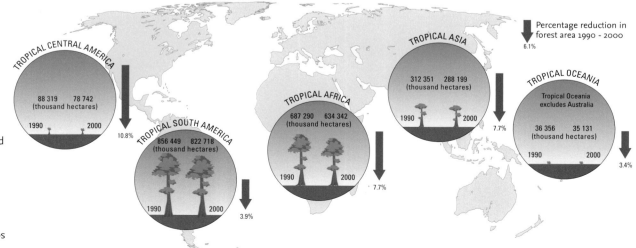

Percentage reduction in forest area 1990 - 2000

**TROPICAL CENTRAL AMERICA**
88 319    78 742
(thousand hectares)
1990    2000
10.8%

**TROPICAL SOUTH AMERICA**
856 449    822 718
(thousand hectares)
1990    2000
3.9%

**TROPICAL AFRICA**
687 290    634 342
(thousand hectares)
1990    2000
7.7%

**TROPICAL ASIA**
312 351    288 199
(thousand hectares)
1990    2000
7.7%

6.1%

**TROPICAL OCEANIA**
Tropical Oceania excludes Australia
36 356    35 131
(thousand hectares)
1990    2000
3.4%

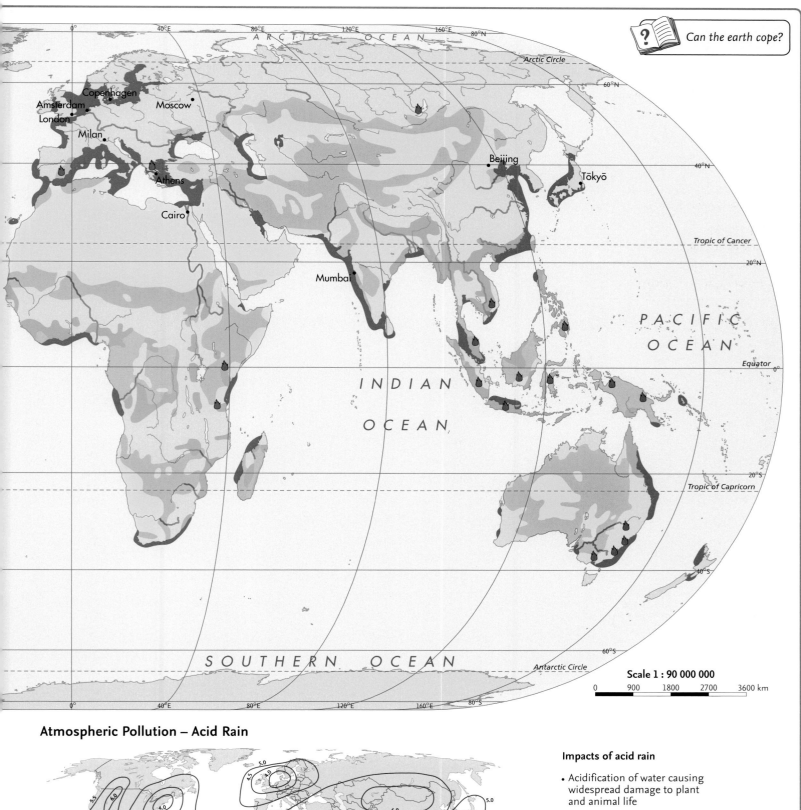

Scale 1 : 90 000 000

0    900    1800    2700    3600 km

## Atmospheric Pollution – Acid Rain

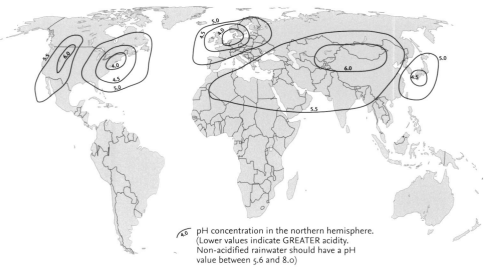

**Impacts of acid rain**

- Acidification of water causing widespread damage to plant and animal life

- Essential nutrients are leached from the soil

- Poor health resulting from toxic metals leached from rocks entering the food chain

- Corrosion of buildings

pH concentration in the northern hemisphere.
(Lower values indicate GREATER acidity.
Non-acidified rainwater should have a pH
value between 5.6 and 8.0)

Eckert IV projection

| Flag | Country | Capital city | Area sq km | Total population 2010 | Density persons per sq km 2010 | Birth rate per 1000 population 2007 | Life expectancy in years 2007 | Population change average % per annum 2005-2010 | Urban population % 2007 |
|---|---|---|---|---|---|---|---|---|---|
| | Afghanistan | Kābul | 652 225 | 28 150 000 | 43 | ... | ... | 3.9 | 24 |
| | Albania | Tirana | 28 748 | 3 155 000 | 110 | 16 | 76 | 0.6 | 46 |
| | Algeria | Algiers | 2 381 741 | 34 895 000 | 15 | 21 | 72 | 1.5 | 65 |
| | Angola | Luanda | 1 246 700 | 18 498 000 | 15 | 47 | 43 | 2.8 | 56 |
| | Antigua & Barbuda | St John's | 442 | 88 000 | 199 | ... | ... | 1.2 | 31 |
| | Argentina | Buenos Aires | 2 766 889 | 40 276 000 | 15 | 18 | 75 | 1.0 | 92 |
| | Armenia | Yerevan | 29 800 | 3 083 000 | 103 | 13 | 72 | -0.2 | 64 |
| | Australia | Canberra | 7 692 024 | 21 293 000 | 3 | 14 | 81 | 1.0 | 89 |
| | Austria | Vienna | 83 855 | 8 364 000 | 100 | 9 | 80 | 0.4 | 67 |
| | Azerbaijan | Baku | 86 600 | 8 832 000 | 102 | 18 | 67 | 0.8 | 52 |
| | Bahamas, The | Nassau | 13 939 | 342 000 | 25 | 17 | 73 | 1.2 | 84 |
| | Bahrain | Manama | 691 | 791 000 | 1 145 | 17 | 76 | 1.8 | 88 |
| | Bangladesh | Dhaka | 143 998 | 162 221 000 | 1 127 | 25 | 64 | 1.7 | 27 |
| | Barbados | Bridgetown | 430 | 256 000 | 595 | 11 | 77 | 0.3 | 39 |
| | Belarus | Minsk | 207 600 | 9 634 000 | 46 | 10 | 70 | -0.6 | 73 |
| | Belgium | Brussels | 30 520 | 10 647 000 | 349 | 11 | 80 | 0.2 | 97 |
| | Belize | Belmopan | 22 965 | 307 000 | 13 | 25 | 76 | 2.1 | 51 |
| | Benin | Porto-Novo | 112 620 | 8 935 000 | 79 | 40 | 57 | 2.8 | 41 |
| | Bhutan | Thimphu | 46 620 | 697 000 | 15 | 18 | 66 | 1.4 | 33 |
| | Bolivia | La Paz/Sucre | 1 098 581 | 9 863 000 | 9 | 27 | 66 | 1.8 | 65 |
| | Bosnia-Herzegovina | Sarajevo | 51 130 | 3 767 000 | 74 | 9 | 75 | 0.1 | 47 |
| | Botswana | Gaborone | 581 370 | 1 950 000 | 3 | 25 | 51 | 1.2 | 59 |
| | Brazil | Brasília | 8 514 879 | 193 734 000 | 23 | 19 | 72 | 1.3 | 85 |
| | Brunei | Bandar Seri Begawan | 5 765 | 400 000 | 69 | 22 | 77 | 2.1 | 74 |
| | Bulgaria | Sofia | 110 994 | 7 545 000 | 68 | 10 | 73 | -0.7 | 71 |
| | Burkina Faso | Ouagadougou | 274 200 | 15 757 000 | 57 | 44 | 52 | 2.9 | 19 |
| | Burundi | Bujumbura | 27 835 | 8 303 000 | 298 | 47 | 49 | 3.9 | 10 |
| | Cambodia | Phnom Penh | 181 000 | 14 805 000 | 82 | 26 | 60 | 1.7 | 21 |
| | Cameroon | Yaoundé | 475 442 | 19 522 000 | 41 | 35 | 50 | 2.0 | 56 |
| | Canada | Ottawa | 9 984 670 | 33 573 000 | 3 | 11 | 81 | 0.9 | 80 |
| | Cape Verde | Praia | 4 033 | 506 000 | 125 | 29 | 71 | 2.2 | 59 |
| | Central African Republic | Bangui | 622 436 | 4 422 000 | 7 | 36 | 45 | 1.8 | 38 |
| | Chad | Ndjamena | 1 284 000 | 11 206 000 | 9 | 45 | 51 | 2.9 | 26 |
| | Chile | Santiago | 756 945 | 16 970 000 | 22 | 15 | 78 | 1.0 | 88 |
| | China | Beijing | 9 584 492 | 1 330 265 000 | 139 | 12 | 73 | 0.6 | 42 |
| | Colombia | Bogotá | 1 141 748 | 45 660 000 | 40 | 19 | 73 | 1.3 | 74 |
| | Comoros | Moroni | 1 862 | 676 000 | 363 | 33 | 65 | 2.5 | 28 |
| | Congo | Brazzaville | 342 000 | 3 683 000 | 11 | 35 | 55 | 2.1 | 61 |
| | Congo, Dem. Rep. of the | Kinshasa | 2 345 410 | 66 020 000 | 28 | 50 | 46 | 3.2 | 33 |
| | Costa Rica | San José | 51 100 | 4 579 000 | 90 | 18 | 79 | 1.5 | 63 |
| | Côte d'Ivoire | Yamoussoukro | 322 463 | 21 075 000 | 65 | 35 | 48 | 1.8 | 48 |
| | Croatia | Zagreb | 56 538 | 4 416 000 | 78 | 9 | 76 | -0.1 | 57 |
| | Cuba | Havana | 110 860 | 11 204 000 | 101 | 10 | 78 | 0.0 | 76 |
| | Cyprus | Nicosia | 9 251 | 871 000 | 94 | 11 | 79 | 1.1 | 70 |
| | Czech Republic | Prague | 78 864 | 10 369 000 | 131 | 11 | 77 | 0.0 | 74 |
| | Denmark | Copenhagen | 43 075 | 547 0000 | 127 | 12 | 78 | 0.2 | 86 |
| | Djibouti | Djibouti | 23 200 | 864 000 | 37 | 29 | 55 | 1.7 | 87 |

... no data available

| Flag | Country | Capital city | Area sq km | Total population 2010 | Density persons per sq km 2010 | Birth rate per 1000 population 2007 | Life expectancy in years 2007 | Population change average % per annum 2005-2010 | Urban population % 2007 |
|---|---|---|---|---|---|---|---|---|---|
|  | Dominica | Roseau | 750 | 67 000 | 89 | ... | ... | -0.3 | 74 |
|  | Dominican Republic | Santo Domingo | 48 442 | 10 090 000 | 208 | 23 | 72 | 1.5 | 68 |
|  | East Timor | Dili | 14 874 | 1 134 000 | 76 | 42 | 61 | 3.5 | 27 |
|  | Ecuador | Quito | 272 045 | 13 625 000 | 50 | 21 | 75 | 1.1 | 65 |
|  | Egypt | Cairo | 1 000 250 | 82 999 000 | 83 | 24 | 71 | 1.8 | 43 |
|  | El Salvador | San Salvador | 21 041 | 6 163 000 | 293 | 23 | 72 | 1.4 | 60 |
|  | Equatorial Guinea | Malabo | 28 051 | 676 000 | 24 | 39 | 52 | 2.4 | 39 |
|  | Eritrea | Asmara | 117 400 | 5 073 000 | 43 | 39 | 58 | 3.2 | 20 |
|  | Estonia | Tallinn | 45 200 | 1 340 000 | 30 | 12 | 73 | -0.4 | 69 |
|  | Ethiopia | Addis Ababa | 1 133 880 | 82 825 000 | 73 | 38 | 53 | 2.5 | 17 |
|  | Fiji | Suva | 18 330 | 849 000 | 46 | 21 | 69 | 0.6 | 52 |
|  | Finland | Helsinki | 338 145 | 5 326 000 | 16 | 11 | 79 | 0.3 | 63 |
|  | France | Paris | 543 965 | 62 343 000 | 115 | 13 | 81 | 0.5 | 77 |
|  | Gabon | Libreville | 267 667 | 1 475 000 | 6 | 26 | 57 | 1.5 | 85 |
|  | Gambia, The | Banjul | 11 295 | 1 705 000 | 151 | 35 | 59 | 2.6 | 56 |
|  | Georgia | T'bilisi | 69 700 | 4 260 000 | 61 | 11 | 71 | -0.8 | 53 |
|  | Germany | Berlin | 357 022 | 82 167 000 | 230 | 8 | 80 | -0.1 | 74 |
|  | Ghana | Accra | 238 537 | 23 837 000 | 100 | 30 | 60 | 2.0 | 49 |
|  | Greece | Athens | 131 957 | 11 161 000 | 85 | 10 | 80 | 0.2 | 61 |
|  | Grenada | St George's | 378 | 104 000 | 275 | 18 | 69 | 0.0 | 31 |
|  | Guatemala | Guatemala City | 108 890 | 14 027 000 | 129 | 33 | 70 | 2.5 | 48 |
|  | Guinea | Conakry | 245 857 | 10 069 000 | 41 | 40 | 56 | 2.2 | 34 |
|  | Guinea-Bissau | Bissau | 36 125 | 1 611 000 | 45 | 50 | 46 | 3.0 | 30 |
|  | Guyana | Georgetown | 214 969 | 762 000 | 4 | 17 | 67 | -0.2 | 28 |
|  | Haiti | Port-au-Prince | 27 750 | 10 033 000 | 362 | 28 | 61 | 1.6 | 45 |
|  | Honduras | Tegucigalpa | 112 088 | 7 466 000 | 67 | 28 | 70 | 2.0 | 47 |
|  | Hungary | Budapest | 93 030 | 9 993 000 | 107 | 10 | 73 | -0.3 | 67 |
|  | Iceland | Reykjavík | 102 820 | 323 000 | 3 | 14 | 81 | 0.8 | 92 |
|  | India | New Delhi | 3 064 898 | 1 198 003 000 | 391 | 24 | 65 | 1.5 | 29 |
|  | Indonesia | Jakarta | 1 919 445 | 229 965 000 | 120 | 19 | 71 | 1.2 | 50 |
|  | Iran | Tehrān | 1 648 000 | 74 196 000 | 45 | 18 | 71 | 1.4 | 68 |
|  | Iraq | Baghdād | 438 317 | 30 747 000 | 70 | ... | ... | 1.8 | 67 |
|  | Ireland | Dublin | 70 282 | 4 515 000 | 64 | 16 | 79 | 1.8 | 61 |
|  | Israel | *Jerusalem | 20 770 | 7 170 000 | 345 | 21 | 81 | 1.7 | 92 |
|  | Italy | Rome | 301 245 | 59 870 000 | 199 | 9 | 81 | 0.1 | 68 |
|  | Jamaica | Kingston | 10 991 | 2 719 000 | 247 | 17 | 73 | 0.5 | 53 |
|  | Japan | Tōkyō | 377 727 | 127 156 000 | 337 | 9 | 83 | 0.0 | 66 |
|  | Jordan | 'Ammān | 89 206 | 6 316 000 | 71 | 29 | 73 | 3.0 | 78 |
|  | Kazakhstan | Astana | 2 717 300 | 15 637 000 | 6 | 20 | 66 | 0.7 | 58 |
|  | Kenya | Nairobi | 582 646 | 39 802 000 | 68 | 39 | 54 | 2.7 | 21 |
|  | Kiribati | Bairiki | 717 | 98 000 | 137 | 27 | 61 | 1.6 | 44 |
|  | Kosovo | Priština | 10 908 | 2 153 139 | 197 | 10 | 73 |  | 52 |
|  | Kuwait | Kuwait | 17 818 | 2 985 000 | 168 | 18 | 78 | 2.4 | 98 |
|  | Kyrgyzstan | Bishkek | 198 500 | 5 482 000 | 28 | 23 | 68 | 1.1 | 36 |
|  | Laos | Vientiane | 236 800 | 6 320 000 | 27 | 27 | 64 | 1.7 | 30 |
|  | Latvia | Rīga | 64 589 | 2 249 000 | 35 | 10 | 71 | -0.5 | 68 |
|  | Lebanon | Beirut | 10 452 | 4 224 000 | 404 | 18 | 72 | 1.1 | 87 |

Jerusalem - not internationally recognised.

... no data available

| Flag | Country | Capital city | Area sq km | Total population 2010 | Density persons per sq km 2010 | Birth rate per 1000 population 2007 | Life expectancy in years 2007 | Population change average % per annum 2005-2010 | Urban population % 2007 |
|------|---------|--------------|-----------|----------------------|-------------------------------|-------------------------------------|-------------------------------|------------------------------------------------|-------------------------|
| | Lesotho | Maseru | 30 355 | 2 067 000 | 68 | 29 | 43 | 0.6 | 25 |
| | Liberia | Monrovia | 111 369 | 3 955 000 | 36 | 50 | 46 | 4.5 | 59 |
| | Libya | Tripoli | 1 759 540 | 6 420 000 | 4 | 23 | 74 | 2.0 | 77 |
| | Liechtenstein | Vaduz | 160 | 36 000 | 225 | ... | ... | 0.9 | 14 |
| | Lithuania | Vilnius | 65 200 | 3 287 000 | 50 | 10 | 71 | -0.5 | 67 |
| | Luxembourg | Luxembourg | 2 586 | 486 000 | 188 | 11 | 79 | 1.1 | 83 |
| | Macedonia | Skopje | 25 713 | 2 042 000 | 79 | 11 | 74 | 0.1 | 66 |
| | Madagascar | Antananarivo | 587 041 | 19 625 000 | 33 | 36 | 59 | 2.7 | 29 |
| | Malawi | Lilongwe | 118 484 | 15 263 000 | 129 | 41 | 48 | 2.6 | 18 |
| | Malaysia | Kuala Lumpur/Putrajaya | 332 965 | 27 468 000 | 82 | 21 | 74 | 1.7 | 69 |
| | Maldives | Male | 298 | 309 000 | 1 037 | 23 | 68 | 1.8 | 37 |
| | Mali | Bamako | 1 240 140 | 13 010 000 | 10 | 48 | 54 | 3.0 | 32 |
| | Malta | Valletta | 316 | 409 000 | 1 294 | 9 | 80 | 0.4 | 94 |
| | Marshall Islands | Dalap-Uliga-Darrit | 181 | 62 000 | 343 | ... | ... | 2.2 | 71 |
| | Mauritania | Nouakchott | 1 030 700 | 3 291 000 | 3 | 32 | 64 | 2.5 | 41 |
| | Mauritius | Port Louis | 2 040 | 1 288 000 | 631 | 14 | 72 | 0.8 | 42 |
| | Mexico | Mexico City | 1 972 545 | 109 610 000 | 56 | 19 | 75 | 1.1 | 77 |
| | Micronesia | Palikir | 701 | 111 000 | 158 | 26 | 69 | 0.5 | 22 |
| | Moldova | Chișinău | 33 700 | 3 604 000 | 107 | 11 | 69 | -0.9 | 42 |
| | Mongolia | Ulan Bator | 1 565 000 | 2 671 000 | 2 | 22 | 67 | 1.0 | 57 |
| | Montenegro | Podgorica | 13 812 | 624 000 | 45 | 14 | 75 | -0.3 | 61 |
| | Morocco | Rabat | 446 550 | 31 993 000 | 72 | 20.5 | 71 | 1.2 | 56 |
| | Mozambique | Maputo | 799 380 | 22 894 000 | 29 | 39.5 | 42 | 2.0 | 36 |
| | Myanmar | Yangôn/Nay Pyi Taw | 676 577 | 50 020 000 | 74 | 18.2 | 62 | 0.9 | 32 |
| | Namibia | Windhoek | 824 292 | 2 171 000 | 3 | 25.7 | 53 | 1.3 | 36 |
| | Nepal | Kathmandu | 147 181 | 29 331 000 | 199 | 28 | 64 | 2.0 | 17 |
| | Netherlands | Amsterdam/The Hague | 41 526 | 16 592 000 | 400 | 11 | 80 | 0.2 | 81 |
| | New Zealand | Wellington | 270 534 | 4 266 000 | 16 | 15 | 80 | 0.9 | 86 |
| | Nicaragua | Managua | 130 000 | 5 743 000 | 44 | 25 | 73 | 1.3 | 56 |
| | Niger | Niamey | 1 267 000 | 15 290 000 | 12 | 49 | 57 | 3.5 | 16 |
| | Nigeria | Abuja | 923 768 | 154 729 000 | 167 | 40 | 47 | 2.3 | 48 |
| | North Korea | P'yŏngyang | 120 538 | 23 906 000 | 198 | 13 | 67 | 0.3 | 62 |
| | Norway | Oslo | 323 878 | 4 812 000 | 15 | 12 | 80 | 0.6 | 77 |
| | Oman | Muscat | 309 500 | 2 845 000 | 9 | 22 | 76 | 2.0 | 72 |
| | Pakistan | Islamabad | 803 940 | 180 808 000 | 225 | 27 | 65 | 1.8 | 36 |
| | Palau | Melekeok | 497 | 20 000 | 40 | 13 | 69 | 0.4 | 79 |
| | Panama | Panama City | 77 082 | 3 454 000 | 45 | 21 | 76 | 1.7 | 72 |
| | Papua New Guinea | Port Moresby | 462 840 | 6 732 000 | 15 | 30 | 57 | 2.0 | 13 |
| | Paraguay | Asunción | 406 752 | 6 349 000 | 16 | 25 | 72 | 1.8 | 60 |
| | Peru | Lima | 1 285 216 | 29 165 000 | 23 | 21 | 71 | 1.2 | 71 |
| | Philippines | Manila | 300 000 | 91 983 000 | 307 | 26 | 72 | 1.9 | 64 |
| | Poland | Warsaw | 312 683 | 38 074 000 | 122 | 10 | 75 | -0.2 | 61 |
| | Portugal | Lisbon | 88 940 | 10 707 000 | 120 | 10 | 78 | 0.4 | 59 |
| | Qatar | Doha | 11 437 | 1 409 000 | 123 | 16 | 76 | 2.1 | 96 |
| | Romania | Bucharest | 237 500 | 21 275 000 | 90 | 10 | 73 | -0.5 | 54 |
| | Russian Federation | Moscow | 17 075 400 | 140 874 000 | 8 | 11 | 68 | -0.5 | 73 |
| | Rwanda | Kigali | 26 338 | 9 998 000 | 380 | 44 | 46 | 2.8 | 18 |
| | St Kitts & Nevis | Basseterre | 261 | 52 000 | 199 | ... | ... | 1.3 | 32 |

... no data available

| Flag | Country | Capital city | Area sq km | Total population 2010 | Density persons per sq km 2010 | Birth rate per 1000 population 2007 | Life expectancy in years 2007 | Population change average % per annum 2005-2010 | Urban population % 2007 |
|---|---|---|---|---|---|---|---|---|---|
| | St Lucia | Castries | 616 | 172 000 | 279 | 14 | 74 | 1.1 | 28 |
| | St Vincent & the Grenadines | Kingstown | 389 | 109 000 | 280 | 20 | 72 | 0.5 | 47 |
| | Samoa | Apia | 2 831 | 163 000 | 58 | 25 | 72 | 0.9 | 23 |
| | São Tomé & Príncipe | São Tomé | 964 | 31 000 | 32 | 32 | 65 | 1.2 | 60 |
| | Saudi Arabia | Riyadh | 2 200 000 | 25 721 000 | 12 | 25 | 73 | 2.2 | 83 |
| | Senegal | Dakar | 196 720 | 12 534 000 | 64 | 35 | 63 | 2.5 | 42 |
| | Serbia | Belgrade | 88 361 | 9 850 000 | 127 | 9 | 73 | 0.1 | 52 |
| | Seychelles | Victoria | 455 | 84 000 | 185 | 18 | 73 | 0.5 | 54 |
| | Sierra Leone | Freetown | 71 740 | 5 696 000 | 79 | 46 | 43 | 2.0 | 37 |
| | Singapore | Singapore | 639 | 4 737 000 | 7 413 | 10 | 80 | 1.2 | 100 |
| | Slovakia | Bratislava | 49 035 | 5 406 000 | 110 | 10 | 74 | 0.0 | 56 |
| | Slovenia | Ljubljana | 20 251 | 2 020 000 | 100 | 10 | 78 | 0.0 | 49 |
| | Solomon Islands | Honiara | 28 370 | 523 000 | 18 | 30 | 64 | 2.3 | 18 |
| | Somalia | Mogadishu | 637 657 | 9 133 000 | 14 | 43 | 48 | 2.9 | 36 |
| | South Africa, Republic of | Pretoria/Cape Town | 1 219 080 | 50 110 000 | 41 | 22 | 50 | 0.6 | 60 |
| | South Korea | Seoul | 99 274 | 48 333 000 | 487 | 10 | 79 | 0.3 | 81 |
| | South Sudan | Juba | 644 329 | 8 260 490 | 13 | ... | ... | ... | ... |
| | Spain | Madrid | 504 782 | 44 904 000 | 89 | 11 | 81 | 0.8 | 77 |
| | Sri Lanka | Sri Jayewardenepura Kotte | 65 610 | 20 238 000 | 308 | 19 | 72 | 0.5 | 15 |
| | Sudan | Khartoum | 1 861 484 | 36 371 510 | 20 | 32 | 59 | 2.2 | 43 |
| | Suriname | Paramaribo | 163 820 | 520 000 | 3 | 19 | 70 | 0.6 | 75 |
| | Swaziland | Mbabane | 17 364 | 1 185 000 | 68 | 29 | 40 | 0.6 | 25 |
| | Sweden | Stockholm | 449 964 | 9 249 000 | 21 | 12 | 81 | 0.5 | 84 |
| | Switzerland | Bern | 41 293 | 7 568 000 | 183 | 10 | 82 | 0.4 | 73 |
| | Syria | Damascus | 185 180 | 21 906 000 | 118 | 27 | 74 | 2.5 | 54 |
| | Taiwan | T'aipei | 36 179 | 23 046 000 | 637 | ... | ... | ... | ... |
| | Tajikistan | Dushanbe | 143 100 | 6 952 000 | 49 | 27 | 67 | 1.5 | 26 |
| | Tanzania | Dodoma | 945 087 | 43 739 000 | 46 | 39 | 52 | 2.5 | 25 |
| | Thailand | Bangkok | 513 115 | 67 764 000 | 132 | 15 | 71 | 0.7 | 33 |
| | Togo | Lomé | 56 785 | 6 619 000 | 117 | 37 | 58 | 2.7 | 41 |
| | Tonga | Nuku'alofa | 748 | 104 000 | 139 | 26 | 73 | 0.5 | 25 |
| | Trinidad & Tobago | Port of Spain | 5 130 | 1 339 000 | 261 | 15 | 70 | 0.4 | 13 |
| | Tunisia | Tunis | 164 150 | 10 272 000 | 63 | 17 | 74 | 1.1 | 66 |
| | Turkey | Ankara | 779 452 | 74 816 000 | 96 | 19 | 72 | 1.3 | 68 |
| | Turkmenistan | Ashgabat | 488 100 | 5 110 000 | 10 | 22 | 63 | 1.3 | 48 |
| | Uganda | Kampala | 241 038 | 32 710 000 | 136 | 47 | 51 | 3.2 | 13 |
| | Ukraine | Kiev | 603 700 | 45 708 000 | 76 | 10 | 68 | -0.8 | 68 |
| | United Arab Emirates | Abu Dhabi | 77 700 | 4 599 000 | 59 | 16 | 79 | 2.9 | 78 |
| | United Kingdom | London | 243 609 | 61 565 000 | 253 | 13 | 79 | 0.4 | 90 |
| | United States of America | Washington | 9 826 635 | 314 659 000 | 32 | 14 | 78 | 1.0 | 81 |
| | Uruguay | Montevideo | 176 215 | 3 361 000 | 19 | 15 | 76 | 0.3 | 92 |
| | Uzbekistan | Tashkent | 447 400 | 27 488 000 | 61 | 21 | 67 | 1.4 | 37 |
| | Vanuatu | Port Vila | 12 190 | 240 000 | 20 | 29 | 70 | 2.4 | 24 |
| | Venezuela | Caracas | 912 050 | 28 583 000 | 31 | 22 | 74 | 1.7 | 93 |
| | Vietnam | Ha Nôi | 329 565 | 88 069 000 | 267 | 19 | 74 | 1.3 | 27 |
| | Yemen | Şan'ā' | 527 968 | 23 580 000 | 45 | 38 | 63 | 3.0 | 30 |
| | Zambia | Lusaka | 752 614 | 12 935 000 | 17 | 39 | 42 | 1.9 | 35 |
| | Zimbabwe | Harare | 390 759 | 12 523 000 | 32 | 28 | 43 | 1.0 | 37 |

... no data available

The important names on the reference maps in the atlas are found in the index. The names are listed in alphabetical order. Each entry gives the country or region of the world in which the name is located followed by the page number, its alphanumeric grid reference and then its co-ordinates of latitude and longitude. Names of very large areas may have these co-ordinates omitted. Area names which are included in the index are referenced to the centre of the feature. In the case of rivers, the mouth or confluence is taken as the point of reference. It is therefore necessary to follow the river upstream from this point to find its name on the map.

On the map of part of Ireland to the right Dublin is found in grid square E3 at latitude 53° 21'N longitude 6° 18'W.

This appears in the index as   **Dublin** Ireland **23 E3** 53.21N 6.18W.   The chart below explains all the elements listed for each entry.

| Dublin | Ireland | 23 | E3 | 53.21N | 6.18W |
|---|---|---|---|---|---|
| Name of the feature to be located. | Name of the country in which the feature is situated. | Page in the atlas where the feature is shown on the largest scale. | Grid square where the feature is found. | Degrees and minutes north or south of the equator. | Degrees and minutes east or west of Greenwich meridian. |

Sometimes an abbreviated description of a feature is included in the entry.
A list of abbreviations used in the index is included below.

## Abbreviations

| | | | | | | | |
|---|---|---|---|---|---|---|---|
| Afghan. | Afghanistan | Dem. Rep. | Democratic Republic of | **Mt.** | Mount | resr. | Reservoir |
| Austa. | Australasia | Congo | the Congo | mtn. | mountain | R.S.A. | Republic of South Africa |
| b., **B.** | bay, Bay | Equat. Guinea | Equatorial Guinea | mts., **Mts.** | mountains | Russian Fed. | Russian Federation |
| Bangla. | Bangladesh | est. | estuary | N. America | North America | Serb. | Serbia |
| Bosnia. | Bosnia-Herzegovina | f. | physical feature eg. valley, | Neth. | Netherlands | S. America | South America |
| c., **C.** | cape, Cape | | plain | N. Korea | North Korea | S. Korea | South Korea |
| C. America | Central America | **G.** | Gulf | **Oc.** | Ocean | str., **Str.** | strait, Strait |
| C.A.R. | Central African Republic | I.o.M | Isle of Man | Pen., **Pen.** | peninsula, Peninsula | Switz. | Switzerland |
| d. | Internal division eg. state, | l. **L.** | lake, Lake | Phil. | Philippines | U.K. | United Kingdom |
| | county | Lux. | Luxembourg | P.N.G. | Papua New Guinea | U.S.A. | United States of America |
| des. | desert | Mont. | Montenegro | r. | river | W. Sahara | Western Sahara |

## A

**Aberdeen** Scotland **22 F4** 57.08N 2.07W
**Aberystwyth** Wales **21 C4** 52.25N 4.06W
**Abidjan** Côte d'Ivoire **48 C5** 5.19N 4.01W
**Abu Dhabi** U.A.E. **36 E3** 24.27N 54.23E
**Abuja** Nigeria **48 D5** 9.12N 7.11E
**Acapulco** Mexico **59 J4** 16.51N 99.56W
**Accra** Ghana **48 C5** 5.33N 0.15W
**Aconcagua, Cerro** mtn. Argentina **63 D3** 32.37S 70.00W
**Adamawa Highlands** Nigeria/Cameroon **48 E5** 7.05N 12.00E
**Adana** Turkey **27 G2** 37.00N 35.19E
**Addis Ababa** Ethiopia **48 G5** 9.03N 38.42E
**Adelaide** Australia **70 D2** 34.56S 138.36E
**Aden, G. of** Indian Oc. **36 D2** 13.00N 50.00E
**Adriatic Sea** Med. Sea **28 F5** 42.30N 16.00E
**Aegean Sea** Med. Sea **26 F2** 39.00N 25.00E
**Afghanistan** Asia **36 F4** 33.00N 65.30E
**Africa** 46–48
**Ahmadabad** India **37 G3** 23.03N 72.40E
**Albania** Europe **26 E3** 41.00N 20.00E
**Aleppo** Syria **36 C4** 36.14N 37.10E
**Alexandria** Egypt **48 F8** 31.13N 29.55E
**Algeria** Africa **48 C7** 28.00N 2.00E
**Algiers** Algeria **48 D8** 36.50N 3.00E
**Alice Springs** Australia **70 D3** 23.42S 133.52E
**Allier** r. France **26 D3** 46.58N 3.04E
**Alps** mts. Europe **26 D3** 46.00N 7.30E
**Altai Mts.** Mongolia **38 B8** 46.30N 93.30E
**Altiplano** f. Bolivia **64 C4** 18.00S 67.30W
**Amazon** r. Brazil **64 F7** 2.00S 50.00W
**Amazon, Mouths of the** f. Brazil **64 G8** 0.00 50.00W
**'Ammān** Jordan **36 C4** 31.57N 35.56E
**Amsterdam** Neth. **26 D4** 52.22N 4.54E
**Amur** r. Russian Fed. **34 J6** 53.17N 140.00E
**Anápolis** Brazil **64 G4** 16.19S 48.58W
**Anchorage** U.S.A. **58 E9** 61.10N 150.00W
**Andaman Is.** India **37 I2** 12.00N 93.00E
**Andaman Sea** Indian Oc. **37 I2** 11.00N 96.00E
**Andes** mts. S. America **62 D5** 15.00S 74.00W
**Andorra** Europe **26 D3** 42.30N 1.32E
**Angola** Africa **49 E3** 12.00S 18.00E
**Ankara** Turkey **27 G2** 39.55N 32.50E
**Anshan** China **38 E8** 41.05N 122.58E
**Antananarivo** Madagascar **49 H3** 18.52S 47.30E

**Antarctica 75**
**Antigua and Barbuda** Lesser Antilles **62 E8** 17.30N 61.49W
**Antofagasta** Chile **63 D4** 23.40S 70.23W
**Aoraki** mtn. New Zealand **71 H1** 43.36S 170.09E
**Apennines** mts. Italy **28 D6** 44.00N 11.00E
**Appalachian Mts.** U.S.A. **59 K6** 39.30N 78.00W
**Arabian Sea** Asia **36 F2** 19.00N 65.00E
**Arafura Sea** Austa. **70 D5** 9.00S 135.00E
**Araguaína** Brazil **64 G6** 7.16S 48.18W
**Araguari** Brazil **64 G4** 18.38S 48.13W
**Aral Sea** Asia **36 E5** 45.00N 60.00E
**Archangel** Russian Fed. **27 H5** 64.32N 41.10E
**Arctic Ocean 74**
**Arequipa** Peru **64 B4** 16.25S 71.32W
**Argentina** S. America **63 E3** 35.00S 65.00W
**Arica** Chile **62 D5** 18.30S 70.20W
**Arkansas** r. U.S.A. **59 J6** 33.50N 91.00W
**Armenia** Asia **36 D5** 40.00N 45.00E
**Arnhem Land** f. Australia **70 D5** 13.00S 132.30E
**Aruba** i. Lesser Antilles **62 D8** 12.30N 70.00W
**Arusha** Tanzania **50 C4** 3.21S 36.40E
**Ashford** England **21 H3** 51.08N 0.53E
**Asia** 34–35
**Asmara** Eritrea **48 G6** 15.20N 38.58E
**Asunción** Paraguay **63 F4** 25.15S 57.40W
**Atacama Desert** S. America **63 D4** 20.00S 69.00W
**Athens** Greece **26 F2** 37.59N 23.42E
**Atlanta** U.S.A. **59 K6** 33.45N 84.23W
**Atlantic Ocean 76 G7**
**Atlas Mts.** Africa **48 C8** 33.00N 4.00W
**Auckland** New Zealand **71 H2** 36.52S 174.45E
**Australia** Austa. **70** 25.00S 135.00E
**Austria** Europe **26 E3** 47.30N 14.00E
**Ayers Rock** see **Uluru** Australia **70**
**Ayr** Scotland **22 D2** 55.28N 4.37W
**Azerbaijan** Asia **36 D5** 40.10N 47.50E
**Azov, Sea of** Ukraine **27 G3** 46.00N 36.30E

## B

**Baffin B.** Canada **58 M10** 74.00N 70.00W
**Baffin I.** Canada **58 L9** 68.50N 70.00W
**Baghdād** Iraq **36 D4** 33.20N 44.26E
**Bahrain** Asia **36 E3** 26.00N 50.35E
**Baikal, L.** Russian Fed. **38 C9** 53.30N 108.00E
**Baja California** pen. Mexico **59 H5** 27.00N 113.00W
**Baku** Azerbaijan **36 D5** 40.22N 49.53E

**Balbina, Represa de** resr. Brazil **64 E7** 1.30S 60.00W
**Balearic Is.** Spain **26 D2** 39.30N 2.30E
**Balkan Mts.** Bulgaria **26 F3** 42.50N 24.30E
**Balkhash, L.** Kazakhstan **34 F6** 46.51N 75.00E
**Baltic Sea** Europe **26 E4** 56.30N 19.00E
**Baltimore** U.S.A. **58 L6** 39.18N 76.38W
**Bamako** Mali **48 C6** 12.40N 7.59W
**Bandar Seri Begawan** Brunei **39 D4** 4.56N 114.58E
**Bangalore** India **37 G2** 12.58N 77.35E
**Bangkok** Thailand **39 C5** 13.45N 100.35E
**Bangladesh** Asia **37 H3** 24.00N 90.00E
**Bangui** C.A.R. **48 E5** 4.23N 18.37E
**Baotou** China **38 D8** 40.38N 109.59E
**Barbados** Lesser Antilles **62 F8** 13.20N 59.40W
**Barcelona** Spain **26 D3** 41.25N 2.10E
**Barents Sea** Arctic Oc. **34 D7** 73.00N 40.00E
**Barquisimeto** Venezuela **62 E8** 10.03N 69.18W
**Barranquilla** Colombia **62 D8** 11.00N 74.50W
**Basel** Switz. **26 D3** 47.33N 7.36E
**Bass Str.** Australia **70 E2** 39.45S 146.00E
**Bath** England **21 E3** 51.22N 2.22W
**Beijing** China **38 D7** 39.55N 116.25E
**Beirut** Lebanon **36 C4** 33.52N 35.30E
**Belarus** Europe **26 F4** 53.00N 28.00E
**Belém** Brazil **64 G7** 1.27S 48.29W
**Belfast** N. Ireland **23 F4** 54.36N 5.57W
**Belgium** Europe **26 D4** 51.00N 4.30E
**Belgrade** Serb. **26 F3** 44.49N 20.28E
**Belize** C. America **59 K4** 17.00N 88.30W
**Belmopan** Belize **59 K4** 17.25N 88.46W
**Belo Horizonte** Brazil **65 H4** 19.45S 43.53W
**Ben Nevis** mtn. Scotland **22 D3** 56.48N 5.00W
**Bengal, B. of** Indian Oc. **37 H2** 17.00N 89.00E
**Benin** Africa **48 D5** 9.00N 2.30E
**Benin, Bight of** b. Africa **48 D5** 5.30N 3.00E
**Bergen** Norway **26 D5** 60.23N 5.20E
**Bering Sea** N. America/Asia **35 N6** 60.00N 170.00W
**Berlin** Germany **26 E4** 52.32N 13.25E
**Bermuda** i. Atlantic Oc. **59 M6** 32.18N 65.00W
**Bern** Switz. **26 D3** 46.57N 7.26E
**Berwick-upon-Tweed** England **20 E7** 55.46N 2.00W
**Bhutan** Asia **37 I3** 27.25N 90.00E
**Bié Plateau** f. Angola **49 E3** 13.00S 16.00E
**Birmingham** England **21 F4** 52.30N 1.55W
**Biscay, B. of** France **26 C3** 45.30N 3.00W
**Bissau** Guinea-Bissau **48 B6** 11.52N 15.39W
**Black Sea** Europe **27 G3** 43.00N 35.00E

**Blackburn** England **20 E5** 53.44N 2.30W
**Blackpool** England **20 D5** 53.48N 3.03W
**Blanc, Mont** mtn. Europe **26 D3** 45.50N 6.52E
**Bogotá** Colombia **62 D7** 4.38N 74.05W
**Bolivia** S. America **62 E5** 17.00S 65.00W
**Bologna** Italy **28 D6** 44.30N 11.20E
**Bolton** England **20 E5** 53.35N 2.26W
**Bombay** see **Mumbai** India **29**
**Bonn** Germany **26 D4** 50.44N 7.06E
**Bordeaux** France **26 C3** 44.50N 0.34W
**Borneo** i. Asia **39 D4** 1.00N 114.00E
**Bosnia-Herzegovina** Europe **26 E3** 44.00N 18.00E
**Boston** U.S.A. **58 L7** 42.15N 71.05W
**Bothnia, G. of** Europe **26 E5** 63.30N 20.30E
**Botswana** Africa **49 F2** 22.00S 24.00E
**Bournemouth** England **21 F2** 50.43N 1.53W
**Bradford** England **20 F5** 53.47N 1.45W
**Brasília** Brazil **64 G4** 15.54S 47.50W
**Bratislava** Slovakia **26 E3** 48.10N 17.10E
**Brazil** S. America **64–65** 10.00S 52.00W
**Brazilian Highlands** Brazil **64 G5** 17.00S 48.00W
**Brazzaville** Congo **48 E4** 4.14S 15.14E
**Brighton** England **21 G2** 50.50N 0.09W
**Brisbane** Australia **70 F3** 27.30S 153.00E
**Bristol** England **21 E3** 51.26N 2.35W
**Bristol Channel** England/Wales **21 C3** 51.17N 3.20W
**British Isles** Europe **24 D5** 54.00N 5.00W
**Brunei** Asia **39 D4** 4.56N 114.58E
**Brussels** Belgium **26 D4** 50.50N 4.23E
**Bucharest** Romania **26 F3** 44.25N 26.06E
**Budapest** Hungary **26 E3** 47.30N 19.03E
**Buenos Aires** Argentina **63 F3** 34.40S 58.30W
**Bujumbura** Burundi **50 A4** 3.22S 29.21E
**Bulgaria** Europe **26 F3** 42.30N 25.00E
**Burkina Faso** Africa **48 C6** 12.15N 1.30W
**Burma** see **Myanmar** Asia **37**
**Bursa** Turkey **26 F3** 40.11N 29.04E
**Burundi** Africa **50 A4** 3.30S 30.00E

## C

**Caernarfon** Wales **20 C5** 53.08N 4.17W
**Cagliari** Italy **28 C3** 39.14N 9.07E
**Cairns** Australia **70 E4** 16.51S 145.43E
**Cairo** Egypt **48 G8** 30.03N 31.15E
**Calais** France **26 D4** 50.57N 1.50E
**Calcutta** see **Kolkata** India **37**
**Calgary** Canada **58 H8** 51.05N 114.05W